EACH ONE
DISCIPLE ONE

stan toler and louie e. bustle

a complete strategy for effective discipleship

BEACON HILL PRESS
OF KANSAS CITY

Copyright 2008
by Stan Toler, Louie E. Bustle, and Beacon Hill Press of Kansas City

ISBN 978-0-8341-2361-8

Printed in the
United States of America

Cover Design: Chad A Cherry/Doug Bennett
Interior Design: Sharon Page

Library of Congress Cataloging-in-Publication Data

Bustle, Louie E. (Louie Elvis), 1942-
  Each one disciple one : a complete strategy for effective discipleship / Louie E. Bustle and Stan Toler.
    p. cm.
  Includes bibliographical references.
  ISBN 978-0-8341-2361-8 (pbk. with resource cd)
  1. Discipling (Christianity) 2. Spiritual formation. I. Toler, Stan. II. Title.

BV4520.B88 2008
253—dc22

                                                                                    2008000971

10 9 8 7 6 5 4 3 2 1

CONTENTS

ABOUT THE AUTHORS

STAN TOLER is a gifted church leader, author, and international speaker with more than 30 years of pastoral ministry experience. Currently senior pastor of Trinity Church of the Nazarene in Oklahoma City, Stan is also executive director of the Toler Leadership Center at Mid-America Christian University. Each year Stan trains thousands of pastors in strategic planning, stewardship, and outreach. He is the author of more than 60 books, including *Each One Win One: A Complete Strategy for Effective Personal Evangelism, ABCs of Evangelism, Lead to Succeed, The Five Star Church, Stan Toler's Practical Guide for Pastoral Ministry, The Cycle of Victorious Giving,* and *Total Quality Life.* Stan and his wife, Linda, have two married sons, Seth and Adam, and live in Oklahoma City.

LOUIE E. BUSTLE is the director of World Mission, Church of the Nazarene. He has been a pastor, district leader, and missionary in the Virgin Islands and served as mission director and first district superintendent of the work he opened in the Dominican Republic. He is the author of numerous articles on holiness and church growth and is coauthor of *Each One Win One: A Complete Strategy for Effective Personal Evangelism.* Louie and his wife, Ellen, have two children, Beth and John, and reside in Shawnee, Kansas.

ACKNOWLEDGMENTS

Special thanks to Jerry Brecheisen, Jim Williams, Annette Ferrell, Pat Diamond, Ellen Bustle, Linda Toler, and Deloris Leonard and also to Bonnie Perry, Barry Russell, Richard Buckner, and the entire Beacon Hill team.

Special thanks to the Bruno Radi family for permission to use materials from his teachings and writings concerning prayer cells.

INTRODUCTION

It isn't necessarily the biggest "names" who make the biggest impact. Just think what Ananias did for Christianity! Ananias, a follower of Jesus Christ in the Early Church, probably wouldn't be interviewed by the network news; he probably wouldn't be the subject of Internet bloggers; and he probably wouldn't be elected to serve on the board of a denomination or a parachurch organization. Little is known about the man, except for his testimony: "He was a devout observer of the law and highly respected by all the Jews living there" (Acts 22:12).

Without this faithful servant of the Lord we might have missed the instruction of the letters to Timothy. The encouragement of the letter to the Philippians wouldn't have been in the Bible. What would our Christian life be without the poignant description of Christ in Colossians? Think how much our lives have been enriched by the writings of Paul the apostle! Ananias was his teacher.

MAKING DISCIPLES

Jesus Christ gave a commission to the church that has not changed over the course of history: "Go and make disciples" (Matt. 28:19). It is one of the most important objectives of the church. In fact, the program of the local church is incomplete without a plan for outreach, and specifically a plan for training new believers in becoming committed disciples of Christ.

Each One Disciple One is a challenge to take on one of the most meaningful assignments of your personal ministry: discipleship. Evangelism is a scriptural priority. Our previous book, *Each One Win One,* outlined a strategy for effective evangelism. *Each One Disciple One* is a strategy for following up those whom you have won.

You will learn to lead a new follower of the Lord Jesus Christ into a meaningful and powerful realm of spiritual discipline and obedience to the Word of God. Your "disciple" will not only learn how to pray and to read the Bible but also learn how to put spiritual skills into practice.

- How to gain by giving
- How to share their faith
- How to have a spiritual influence in the home

Discipleship is at the very core of vibrant Christianity. Jesus had disciples—learners who applied His principles in such a way that the whole world was affected. Whether you are conducting a small group or meeting one-on-one, the principles of *Each One Disciple One* will give you the necessary tools for impacting the lives of others.

NEW DISCIPLE TO A DISCIPLER

The book is divided into three sections. *Section One* is for the new disciple. There are eight disciplines that every follower of Jesus Christ practices: pursuing holiness, private worship, public worship, observing the sacraments, witnessing, discipling, stewardship, and church membership. This section can be used by the discipler to teach a class, for meeting one-on-one with disciples, or as curriculum for a small-group study.

Section Two is a challenge to become a discipler. It will give you the vision, strategy, and methods for helping others grow in their faith—including their pursuit of holiness. Each chapter includes proven principles for leading new Christians from Point A to Point B and beyond. You will learn how to multiply your ministry through others by using the D-I-S-C-I-P-L-E plan. Your discipler will learn how to teach others to be "disciplers"—how to develop disciples with a vision of outreach and church planting. It incorporates eight objectives into the discipling process:

- Developing intentional friendships
- Identifying the disciple's spiritual understanding level
- Supplying a support system for the disciple
- Contacting disciples regarding spiritual progress/needs
- Incorporating disciples into the life/ministries of the church
- Praying daily for the disciple's spiritual growth
- Looking for the disciple's spiritual gifts
- Enlisting the disciple in ministry

Section Three is a toolbox for disciplers. It includes lesson study guides, practical giveaways for individuals or groups, and in-hand resources for new Christians. It also includes strategies for church planting and church growth. Many of the resources in Section Three are also included on the *Each One Disciple One* CD for reference, duplication, or adaptation by the local church.

ONE PERSON AT A TIME

Every page is dedicated to assisting you in building the Kingdom one person at a time. It is our prayer that God will use this material—and most of all use you—to strengthen believers in their faith and cast a vision for church multiplication.

—Stan Toler and Louie E. Bustle

SECTION ONE

BECOMING A DISCIPLE

① PURSUING HOLINESS

Every successful person sets goals. Whether in business, sports, or ministry, someone who has reached the next level has determined to get there. It's the same in your spiritual journey with God.

You began your journey:

- You saw your need (Rom. 7:18-20).
- You trusted God to give you a new start (2 Cor. 5:17).
- You confessed your sinful disobedience against His will and His Word (1 John 1:9).
- You prayed and invited God's only Son, the Lord Jesus Christ, into your life (Rev. 3:20).
- You believed that He forgave you of your past (Rom. 10:9-10).
- You promised to live a new life of faith in Him (Gal. 2:20).
- You set out to do *what it takes* to be *what He wants you to be* (Phil. 3:11-12).

1. GROWING

The New Testament writer Peter suggests that you keep *going* by *growing:* "Grow in the grace and knowledge of our Lord and Savior Jesus Christ" (2 Pet. 3:18). Do you see the two components of that growth? First, "grow in the grace." Your spiritual growth comes from the strength, direction, and affirmation God gives to you. "Grace" means that it is a gift. You can't earn it. You can't buy it. You rely on God for it. God simply gives you the supplies to be more like Him, upon your request.

2. LEARNING

The second component describes your part: to grow in "the knowledge of our Lord and Savior Jesus Christ." How do you grow in knowledge? You discipline yourself to study and to put into practice what you learn from His Word: "Do your best to present yourself to God as one approved, a workman who does not need to be ashamed and who correctly handles the word of truth" (2 Tim. 2:15). A "workman" works. And work takes discipline: "No one serving as a soldier gets involved in civilian affairs—he wants to please his commanding officer. Similarly, if anyone competes as an athlete, he does not receive the victor's crown unless he competes according to the rules. The hardworking farmer should be the first to receive a share of the crops" (vv. 4-6).

3. PERFECTING

Each of the illustrations used by the apostle—the soldier, the athlete, and the farmer—describes someone who has a great amount of focus, dedication, and determination. They "pursue perfection." That doesn't mean they are perfect in all of their actions; it simply means they are "perfect" in their direction and in their intention. They pursue "doing" and "being" the best they can. The soldier focuses on physical fitness, military technique, and weaponry to carry out orders from a commanding officer. The athlete focuses not only on physical fitness but also on agility and practice to push his or her body to the very limit. The farmer focuses on planting, tending, and harvesting what has been sown, using all the right tools in the process.

The soldier, the athlete, and the farmer may have every supply necessary to accomplish their tasks, but without disciplined and diligent efforts, they will fall short of their goals. What is your goal? God has already spelled it out in the Bible:

> Prepare your minds for action; be self-controlled; set your hope fully on the grace to be given you when Jesus Christ is revealed. As obedient children, do not conform to the evil desires you had when you lived in ignorance. But just as he who called you is holy, so be holy in all you do; for it is written: "Be holy, because I am holy" *(1 Pet. 1:13-16).*

4. DEDICATION

God wants you to be spiritually complete, to be "wholly holy." You are called to be like Him in your attitude and actions. What does that look like? It looks like the life of Jesus: "Your attitude should be the same as that of Christ Jesus" (Phil. 2:5). You are a follower of Christ—a Christian (Christ-one, one of Christ's), one who seeks to be like Him in everything you do. You are His "disciple" (learner, follower). You are dedicated to obeying Him and learning how to be like Him.

Dedication is a mark of excellence. In the sports world, for example, golfer Tiger Woods may be the greatest of all time. His long golf drives from the tee, his skill in chipping the golf ball onto the green, and his accuracy in putting that ball into the hole have made him a very successful athlete. But his skill didn't just happen. He spent untold numbers of hours practicing. He drove golf balls on the driving range. He practiced chipping the golf ball up to the green. He learned how to line up the ball with the hole and putt with accuracy. He disciplined himself to play the game of golf—within the boundaries of the rules of golf.

You may not be the greatest golfer in the world, but you can practice like one. You can work on driving the golf ball, hitting it off the tee time after time, day after day. You can learn the "feel" of the golf club as you diligently practice the short strokes of "chipping" the ball onto the green. You can learn to line up the golf ball to putt it into the hole, and then practice putting it—hour after hour. And you can learn to live by the "rules of the game."

Likewise, you may not be considered the greatest Christian that ever lived, but you can practice like one.

- You can discipline your mind to learn everything you can about Christ and the Bible.
- You can copy Him in your love and service to others.
- You can "line up" your heart with the principles He taught and "aim" to live by them.
- You can determine to live by the rules written in the Bible. In fact, you can be the best follower of Christ you can be!
- You can pursue holiness.

5. ASSURANCE

What is involved in that pursuit? First, be certain of your salvation. When you received Christ into your heart as an act of faith, you were saved from being lost (Titus 3:5-7). You were away from God, your sin (breaking His law on purpose: "Everyone who sins breaks the law; in fact, sin is lawlessness" [1 John 3:4]) had separated you from Him. And breaking the law meant paying the penalty: "The wages of sin is death" (Rom. 6:23a). You were spiritually dead—dead to God's will (His purpose for your life) and to the Word of God (His written rules and promises). You deserved the "wage" (penalty) of (spiritual) death. But God loved you so much He provided a way back to Him—a way of life. He paid the price for your salvation from being lost by offering His only Son, Jesus, as your representative:

"The gift of God is eternal life in Christ Jesus our Lord" (Rom. 6:23b). It was as if a judge in a court of law had pronounced a death sentence and then was executed on behalf of the prisoner.

At the moment you told God how sorry you were for disobeying His will and His Word and asked Jesus Christ to come into your life and to be the Lord of your life (you repented; that is, you turned away from sin and to God), every act of disobedience was forgiven—and forgotten: "I will forgive their wickedness and will remember their sins no more" (Heb. 8:12).

Perhaps you've been in a large shopping center and suddenly realized you didn't know where you were. And perhaps you remember looking at a sign posted that had a map on it; and on the map there was a large *X* with the words "You are here." There are several "signs" that give you the assurance that you have been found—that you have been saved from being lost.

- *God's promise.* God cannot lie. It is against His very character: "Paul, a servant of God and an apostle of Jesus Christ for the faith of God's elect and the knowledge of the truth that leads to godliness—a faith and knowledge resting on the hope of eternal life, which God, *who does not lie,* promised before the beginning of time" (Titus 1:1-2, emphasis added). You can be sure that you have been saved from being lost—that you are a child of God by faith in the Lord Jesus Christ—because God said you are (John 1:12).

- *The Holy Spirit's witness.* God the Holy Spirit teaches us about God the Son (John 15:1-16). He reveals Christ's power and purpose in the Christian believer's heart (Rom. 8:11). He also came to give us the assurance that we belong to God: "The Spirit himself testifies with our spirit that we are God's children" (v. 16). It is the Holy Spirit who gives you the assurance that your guilt is forgiven and that you have peace with God.

- *Fruit of the Spirit.* When you plant something—a tree or a crop, for example—you expect it to show evidence of what it is, as it grows. The Holy Spirit produces "evidence" in your life that you belong to God through faith in the Lord Jesus Christ; that you have begun to grow in Him. That evidence is displayed in your attitude and in your actions: "But the fruit of the Spirit is love, joy, peace, patience, kindness, goodness, faithfulness, gentleness and self-control" (Gal. 5:22-23a). You have a new "self" inwardly that is revealed outwardly.

- *Change of direction.* Another indication that you are saved is the difference your faith has made in your life. "Therefore, if anyone is in Christ, he is a new creation; the old has gone, the new has come!" (2 Cor. 5:17). Your priorities have changed. You want to be with other Christians. You have a new interest in reading the Bible. Church attendance has a new meaning. Now, prayer is more than saying grace before a meal—you want to talk with God.

- *Desire for service.* As a new "Christ-one" (Christian) you see things in a different light—God's light: Wherever you see a need, you want to help meet the need. You want to do His work.

> Jesus went through all the towns and villages, teaching in their synagogues, preaching the good news of the kingdom and healing every disease and sickness. When he saw the crowds, he had compassion on them, because they were harassed and helpless, like sheep without a shepherd. Then he said to his disciples, "The harvest is plentiful but the workers are few. Ask the Lord of the harvest, therefore, to send out workers into his harvest field" *(Matt. 9:35-38).*

> Jesus brought that compassion with Him into your heart. You have a desire to minister to the helpless and hurting. You have a desire to share with others what God has done for you. You want to answer God's call for "workers." That very interest is a sign that you belong to Him.

13

- *Hunger for holiness.* As you learn and obey God's Word, you will soon want everything that God has to offer—and you will soon realize that God has even more for you. You will want to keep pursuing a holy life. (Remember, that is what He called you to do: 1 Pet. 1:13-16.) As you continue to pursue holiness, you will discover areas of your life that you can turn over to Him. You will even come to a point where you will make a decision to turn every area of your life over to Him (an experience subsequent to being saved, called sanctification—being "set apart" for holy use).

6. REACHING

As we said, as a Christian you have a goal God has given you. You are to pursue holiness. By faith, you invited Jesus to come into your life. And by faith, you can ask Him to take full control of your life. As an example, imagine that you are showing Jesus through the "home" of your heart. Imagine taking Him to every room—pointing out the things you think are of most importance. You have made Him feel welcome in your "home."

But imagine taking that welcome a step farther. During the "tour" you discovered some things that needed fixing (e.g., you discovered rebellion, selfishness, or desires for the things of your past). Some things just didn't fit in your "home" since you have become a Christian. You need an extreme makeover. You decide the best way is not to just ask Jesus to do "repairs" but to take ownership: you decide to give Him your "home" and let Him do what needs to be done with it. The Bible tells us about that experience: "I urge you . . . in view of God's mercy, to offer your bodies as living sacrifices, holy and pleasing to God—this is your spiritual act of worship" (Rom. 12:1).

You are certain of your salvation, and you are certain you want everything God has to offer. You are reaching. You are obeying Him. You are surrendering to His will for your life. And you have a desire to be completely His. Congratulations! You have started on a great adventure: pursuing holiness.

② PRIVATE WORSHIP

A "time-out" is a disciplined act of stopping what you are doing and focusing on something else. All disciples (learners, followers) of Jesus Christ need a daily, spiritual time-out; a time to reflect on what God *has* done, *is* doing, and *will* do for them. A time of spiritual rest. A time to think spiritual thoughts. A time to change spiritual directions.

A time of private worship—away from the busyness or the noise of the day—is a must for every growing Christian. "But what do I do during that time out?" you might ask. There are at least five key ingredients in a daily time of private worship.

1. PRAYER

Every relationship begins with communication. Prayer is a communications link between people and God. It is as simple as talking. Prayer expresses your love for God and your dependence on Him to supply your daily needs—physical, spiritual, social, financial, and emotional.

Let's take a look at this important part of your private worship.

a. What is prayer?

Of all the questions the followers of Jesus could have asked Him while He was on the earth, they chose to ask Him about prayer: "And it came to pass, that, as he was praying in a certain place, when he ceased, one of his disciples said unto him, Lord, teach us to pray" (Luke 11:1, KJV). Maybe you have questions about prayer.

(1) **Prayer is talking to God.** It is the greatest "open door policy" of all: God, the Ruler of the universe, invites you to enter the "throne room of heaven" and talk to Him about anything you have on your heart. "Let us then approach the throne of grace with confidence, so that we may receive mercy and find grace to help us in our time of need" (Heb. 4:16).

(2) **Prayer is responding to God.** Communication also involves listening. God not only wants to watch over you and provide for you but also wants to give you daily instructions. Effective praying involves good listening. God said to His people, Israel, "Hear, O Israel, and be careful to obey so that it may go well with you and that you may increase greatly" (Deut. 6:3).

How does He speak to you? He speaks in at least four ways:

- *He speaks to you through the Bible.* The Bible was written to be your map through life: "Your word is a lamp to my feet and a light for my path" (Ps. 119:105). As you walk in its "light," you walk safely and securely.
- *He speaks to you inwardly.* God will use your reason and your conscience to give you direction and affirmation. "When he, the Spirit of truth, comes, he will guide you into all truth" (John 16:13).
- *He speaks to you through the counsel of other Christians.* The godly advice of other Christians is another way that God gives you instruction, confidence, or warning. "The lips of the righteous nourish many" (Prov. 10:21).
- *He speaks to you through circumstances.* God even uses the open and closed doors of life to guide us: "And we know that in all things God works for the good of those who love him, who have been called according to his purpose" (Rom. 8:28).

b. Why should I pray?

The reasons for prayer are as many as the experiences of your life. Here are several:

(1) You pray to express a need. Jesus said, "I tell you the truth, my Father will give you whatever you ask in my name. . . . Ask and you will receive, and your joy will be complete" (John 16:23b-24). God loves you and wants to supply your needs according to His will (Luke 11).

(2) You pray for forgiveness of sin. Disobeying the written laws of God (in the Bible) on purpose is sin. You don't have to sin. You can choose to live by God's law. But if you sin, you have a promised source of forgiveness. "If we confess our sins, he is faithful and just and will forgive us our sins and purify us from all unrighteousness" (1 John 1:9).

(3) You pray for healing. The God who formed you (Ps. 139:13) is able to restore you. "Is any one of you sick? He should call the elders of the church to pray over him and anoint him with oil in the name of the Lord. And the prayer offered in faith will make the sick person well" (James 5:14-15). God answers your prayer according to His loving purpose for your life—and in response to your faith.

(4) You pray for the needs of others. The apostle Paul said, "In all my prayers for all of you, I always pray with joy" (Phil. 1:4). As a Christian you are an "intercessor," a go-between. You bring the spiritual, physical, financial, or social needs of others to God in prayer, asking on their behalf.

(5) You pray for the increase of God's kingdom. You want people everywhere to know about Christ and His offer of salvation. You pray that missionaries will be sent to those who are lost without Christ (John 14:6). And you pray that God will help you to be a part of that effort.

(6) You pray for community and national leaders. "I urge, then, first of all, that requests, prayers, intercession and thanksgiving be made for everyone—for kings and all those in authority, that we may live peaceful and quiet lives in all godliness and holiness" (1 Tim. 2:1-2).

c. When should I pray?

You will know the best time of the day for you to have your daily private worship. Here are some considerations to keep in mind:

- Are you a morning person or a night person?
- What part of the day seems to be less hectic?
- When will you be less interrupted by the schedules of others in the home?

d. Where should you pray?

It may be difficult, but find someplace where you are alone. Whether indoors or outdoors, it should be a place where you can spend time alone with God. See the example in Jesus' life: "After the people saw the miraculous sign that Jesus did, they began to say, 'Surely this is the Prophet who is to come into the world.' Jesus, knowing that they intended to come and make him king by force, withdrew again to a mountain by himself" (John 6:14-15). Jesus often prayed alone, in a mountain setting.

e. How should I pray?

Remember, prayer is talking to God; it is a natural conversation. There are no required words. There isn't a set regimen, but having a basic "pattern" for prayer will help focus your attention. Again, Jesus gave us an example in Matt. 6:9-14. From those verses, one of the most familiar prayers in Christianity, the Lord's Prayer, was formed, and an outline of that prayer will give you a prayer pattern.

(1) "Our Father, who art in heaven, hallowed be thy Name."

Begin your prayer by praising God, thanking Him for who He is, as revealed in the Bible, and for what He has done for you today or in the past (days, weeks, months).

(2) **"Thy Kingdom come, thy will be done, on earth as it is in heaven."**

Pray for God's will to be done in your life and in the world (in your home, in your place of employment, in the lives of your family, in your church, and in your nation and in the lives of its leaders—pray that God will have first place).

(3) **"Give us this day our daily bread."**

Present your daily needs to God (called petition) and ask Him to meet them individually—spiritual, physical, financial, family—according to His will; present your needs for the day and the needs of others—friends, family, coworkers, missionaries, pastors, national leaders, hospitalized or ill, grieving or lonely, troubled or financially needy—and ask God to meet their needs according to His will (called intercession).

(4) **"Forgive us our trespasses, as we forgive those who trespass against us."**

Ask God to forgive any willful (on purpose) sin in your life. Also, ask God to forgive any deeds or actions committed by others against you.

(5) **"Lead us not into temptation, but deliver us from evil."**

Pray for God's power and wisdom to help you face areas where you are spiritually vulnerable (temptations).

(6) **"Thine is the kingdom, and the power, and the glory, for ever and ever. Amen."**[1]

Praise God that He is in control of your life and in control of everything around you. Thank Him for being faithful to you; for loving you, and for forgiving you.

2. BIBLE READING

The second ingredient for your time of private worship is Bible reading. Samuel Logan Brengle, a classic Christian author and a commissioner in The Salvation Army, wrote an article titled "How to Study the Bible." His love for God's Word was evident from the beginning instructions:

> Read and study it as two young lovers read and study each other's letters. As soon as the mail brings a letter from his sweetheart, the young man grabs it and without waiting to see if there is not another letter for him, runs off to a corner and reads and laughs and rejoices over it and almost devours it. . . . He meditates on it day and night, and reads it over again and then again.[2]

a. What is the Bible?

In one sense, the Bible (meaning "book") is a library. It contains 66 different "books" and letters, written under the inspiration of the Holy Spirit by over 40 authors, during a span of 1,600 years. It is divided into two sections: the Old Testament and the New Testament.

b. Why read the Bible?

The Bible itself speaks of its benefits in 2 Tim. 3:16-17 (NKJV): "All Scripture is given by inspiration of God, and is profitable for doctrine, for reproof, for correction, for instruction in righteousness, that the man of God may be complete, thoroughly equipped for every good work."

(1) **Because it is the inspired Word of God:** "All Scripture is given by inspiration of God . . ." "Inspired" means "God-breathed." In other words, God the Holy Spirit "breathed" His message into the minds and hearts of those who wrote it down and translated it for our understanding. Since God is eternal, His Word is eternally relevant.

(2) **Because it teaches us basic doctrines (beliefs):** ". . . and is profitable for doctrine . . ." As Christ's disciple it is important to have a good foundation of belief (1 Pet. 3:15). There are many teach-

ers—of many religions—so it is important to know what is true and what is false. God's Word, the Bible, is true: "All your words are true; all your righteous laws are eternal" (Ps. 119:160). It addresses at least three important areas of truth:

- Where we came from (creation)
- Why we are here (purpose)
- Where we are going after we die (eternity)

(3) **Because it teaches us how to live:** ". . . for reproof, for correction, for instruction in righteousness . . ." God loves us so much that He gave us an "Owner's Manual." God has given you instructions on how to live—and maintain—your life for Him. Life can be difficult at times. We need the directions.

(4) **Because it gives us a sense of belonging:** ". . . that the man of God may be complete . . ." No matter your gender, age, race, origin, or economic condition, God wants you to belong to Him— and know it. First John 5:19-20 says:

> We know that we are children of God, and that the whole world is under the control of the evil one. We know also that the Son of God has come and has given us understanding, so that we may know him who is true. And we are in him who is true—even in his Son Jesus Christ. He is the true God and eternal life.

(5) **Because it tells how to serve God:** ". . . thoroughly equipped for every good work." You will have opportunities every day to share God's love with others. But how? What should you say? What should you do? The Bible is a blueprint for constructing a lifestyle that will make you a good—and godly—influence.

c. How to read the Bible

Let's look again at Brengle's "How to Study the Bible" for some guidelines on reading the Bible and applying them to private worship times.[3]

- **"Read and study it as two young lovers read and study each other's letters."** Read it with anticipation that God will reveal His eternal love for you in the words you will read. Pray before you read.
- **"Read . . . what the disciples in Berea did."** (Berea was the location of a church in New Testament times.) God's Word says Christians in Berea accepted the teachings of Christ's teachers "with great eagerness and examined the Scriptures every day to see if what Paul said was true" (Acts 17:11). Read it with an open mind. Be willing to accept its truth. Study it. Read the Scripture verses over again. Use study helps (commentaries, notes in a study Bible, modern versions, etc.).
- **"Read and study the word not to get a mass of knowledge in the head, but a flame of love in the heart."** Read it with an eagerness to do what it says to do—and be what it says to be. Let it inspire you to spiritual greatness!
- **"Follow carefully the line of thought from verse to verse and chapter to chapter."** That is, have a system of study. For example, read through the Bible, one book at a time, over the course of a year. Study each chapter of the book. Then look at each verse of the chapter. Journal your reading, asking yourself of each chapter or verse:

  "What is the subject?"
  "What should I learn?"
  "What stands out to me?"
  "Who is it talking about?"
  "What does it tell me to do?"

"What does it tell me not to do?"

"What is God saying to me?"

3. INCLUDE A DEVOTIONAL BOOK

There is no substitute for the Bible: "Faith comes by hearing, and hearing by the word of God" (Rom. 10:17, NKJV). However, including a daily devotional book along with your Bible reading is an added dimension.

a. What devotional book should I read?

Some of the most well-known daily devotional books include *My Utmost for His Highest* by Oswald Chambers, *Streams in the Desert* by Mrs. Charles E. Cowman, and *Morning and Evening* by Charles Haddon Spurgeon. A daily devotional book usually highlights a Bible verse and then makes a brief application of the verse for daily living.

Christian bookstores and Christian Web sites will offer not only the classics but also more contemporary devotionals. Your denomination's publishing house will have an extensive list of books that will give you inspirational insights and quotes that will reinforce your daily Bible readings. Also, your pastor or Bible study leader may recommend a favorite devotional book for your private worship times.

b. When should I read?

You could read a daily devotional following your prayer and Bible reading, or you could read it as a stand-alone book at another time of the day. The Holy Spirit may "highlight" a sentence from your daily devotional reading that will be exactly what you need for the day—or exactly what you need to answer some question about your own faith journey.

4. MEDITATION

Your spiritual time-out will also be enhanced by spending time in meditation. Christian meditation is vastly different from the meditation associated with other religions. Meditation that doesn't focus on God and His Word makes you spiritually vulnerable.

You have changed your thinking to allow Jesus Christ to direct you. Emptying your mind of any thought—especially thoughts of God—allows a place for the enemy of your faith, the devil (1 Pet. 5:8), to insert his rebellious thoughts against God.

Christian meditation may include thinking on a verse of scripture, or words from a verse, that have been part of your Bible reading—letting God's Word "soak into your inner person" like water soaks the soil.

5. PRAISE

The writers of the Old Testament Psalms reflected on God's presence in a time of worship: "Enter his gates with thanksgiving and his courts with praise; give thanks to him and praise his name" (Ps. 100:4). Private worship that includes time of praise is quality worship.

What is praise?

Praise is reflecting on God's character, goodness, and faithfulness. It expresses out loud what you feel inside. For example, it is a time to tell Jesus how much you love Him. It is a time to express your gratitude to Him for what He has done for you (dying on the Cross on behalf of you, paying the penalty for your sins, forgiving you of your past, and giving you a hope for the future). "Let the word of

Christ dwell in you richly as you teach and admonish one another with all wisdom, and as you sing psalms, hymns and spiritual songs with gratitude in your hearts to God" (Col. 3:16). Just as the content of your praise may be varied, so your "format" of praise may vary:

- Listening to Christian music
- Singing a song
- Meditating on God's goodness
- Reading hymns or songs

"Worship" comes from the root word meaning "worthiness." The dictionary defines it as "reverence offered a divine being or supernatural power; also: an act of expressing such reverence."[4] The benefit of private worship times will not only enrich your faith journey but also give you a more positive outlook and a greater spiritual influence.

③ PUBLIC WORSHIP

John Wesley once said that no true Christian will ever go to heaven alone. Christians need each other. Private worship is important, but it is also important to worship with other Christians in a church setting. The church setting may differ from a small building to a large auditorium to the living room of a house, but the Scriptures almost always speak of believers in a group setting. In fact, believers are encouraged to meet together for times of fellowship and public worship: "Let us not give up meeting together, as some are in the habit of doing, but let us encourage one another" (Heb. 10:25). Public worship is vital to your spiritual growth.

In the New Testament, the word translated "church" is found over 100 times. And in over 90 of those instances the word refers to a group of Christians in a particular location—in other words "local churches." In the beginnings of the church era, the disciples of Jesus Christ either found a place of public worship when they arrived in a place or they started one. It should be the same today. Attending a church where the Bible is respected—and taught—is important to your faith journey. Christian churches were formed to provide a place to meet the spiritual needs of their attendees.

1. THE IMPORTANCE OF THE CHURCH

There are several reasons for attending a local church, each important to you for spiritual growth. You need the church.

a. You need the nourishment of the church.

The local church provides a place where your spiritual growth is nourished. It is a place where you can be fed spiritually. You need its Bible messages and teaching. You need its fellowship and counsel. In the physical, diets that lack the right foods promote sickness and disease. If you want to keep fit spiritually, you will pay attention to your spiritual diet. Jesus said, "Do not work for food that spoils, but for food that endures to eternal life" (John 6:27).

b. You need the guidance of the church.

As a river needs banks to channel its energy and direction, you need the "banks" of a local church for spiritual energy and direction. Hebrews 13:17 says, "Obey your leaders and submit to their authority. They keep watch over you as men who must give an account." The prayerful concern of fellow believers in the local church setting may keep you from making the wrong life decisions. The combined wisdom of fellow Christians is a great source of knowledge and help.

c. You need the ministry of the church.

Vocational and lay ministers in the local church have been gifted to care for you spiritually.

> But to each one of us grace has been given as Christ apportioned it. . . . It was he who gave some to be apostles, some to be prophets, some to be evangelists, and some to be pastors and teachers, to prepare God's people for works of service, so that the body of Christ may be built up until we all reach unity in the faith and in the knowledge of the Son of God and become mature, attaining to the whole measure of the fullness of Christ *(Eph. 4:7, 11-13)*.

Those gifts are seen in the church's public worship.

You also need the ministry of the church in transition times. The ministry of the church will assist you with prayer, counsel, encouragement, and teaching to help you—and your family—through difficult times. It will share in the joy of your baptism or wedding ceremony. And it will share in the grief of a funeral service.

d. You need the activities of the church.

The church has scheduled activities that will assist you in your faith journey. Its worship times will lift your spirits and help you to focus on God. Its teaching times will give you insights from the Bible and practical applications for growing intellectually. Its group studies will give you a sense of family and help you network with people who share your beliefs. The church is called a body. Its parts function in harmony with each other and, together, draw holiness and help from the Head of the Church—Christ. First Corinthians 12:27 says, "Now you are the body of Christ, and each one of you is a part of it."

e. You need the fellowship of the church.

Public worship is a place where you can meet people of all ages and interests but who share the same faith. You need the friendship of other Christians. You need the church's informal times. You need its varied activities. You need the assurance that you have brothers and sisters in faith who will not only help you when needed but also give help to your family members. "We proclaim to you what we have seen and heard, so that you also may have fellowship with us. And our fellowship is with the Father and with his Son, Jesus Christ" (1 John 1:3).

f. You need the administration of the church.

You are a steward (manager) of God's resources: "The earth is the LORD's, and everything in it, the world, and all who live in it" (Ps. 24:1). As one of Christ's disciples you have a responsibility to use those resources wisely. The administration of the local church (its organization) gives you opportunity to use your time, treasures, and talents in a resourceful way—a way that honors Christ and helps others to know about Him.

2. THE WORSHIP OF THE CHURCH

Public worship is more than an activity; it is an experience. God inhabits the worship of His people. His joy flows through every expression of praise. His love overshadows every corporate concern. His power flows through every spoken word. When you meet together with other spiritual seekers, you are being strengthened by their strength; and their weaknesses challenge you to become spiritually fit. Also, worship is putting words and actions to your thanksgiving for God's goodness. "Ascribe to the LORD the glory due his name. Bring an offering and come before him; worship the LORD in the splendor of his holiness" (1 Chron. 16:29).

Public worship is not a spectator sport. It is a time to actively express your love for God—and your faith in Him—by participating in the worship service: singing, serving, giving, sharing, and learning.

a. Singing

Singing songs of worship is a practice that goes all the way back to Old Testament times. In fact, the Old Testament psalms were used as song lyrics. Before there were local churches, believers in God met in large temples or tabernacles. In New Testament times, public worship was often conducted in smaller settings—and often in houses. But no matter the size or the ceremony, singing was always a vital part of worship.

You may not have a great singing voice, or may not even be able to carry a tune, but your participation in the singing is an important worship activity.

b. Serving

Psalm 100:2 (NKJV) says, "Serve the LORD with gladness; come before His presence with singing." Public worship gives you not only an opportunity to praise God but also an opportunity to use your talents in service to Him. In worship, many gifts are displayed:

- Preaching
- Teaching
- Singing
- Playing an instrument
- Acting in a drama

But not all of the worship participants are on the platform or stage. Many have gifts that are used behind the scenes. Their service is part of and contributes to the overall worship experience:

- Ushers
- Greeters
- Cleaning or setup crew
- Worship arts technician
- Children's church worker
- Nursery worker

c. Giving

The Bible says, "Give to the LORD the glory due His name; bring an offering, and come into His courts" (Ps. 96:8, NKJV). Giving to the Lord is as much a part of the public worship service as anything else. In most worship services there is a time when an offering is received. Christians contribute to that offering out of delight and not duty—they are delighted to obey the Lord in the giving of their tithes and offerings. "Tithe" means "tenth." Tithing is the act of giving a percentage of your income back to the Lord—through the local church. It is the biblical standard for giving—not some organization's standard (Mal. 3:10). Offerings are "bonus" gifts—above the tithe.

d. Sharing

The sharing times of public worship include more than giving a monetary gift. You can give of yourself through fellowship. The Bible speaks of ways we can interact with others through the activities of the church:

- Showing acceptance (Rom. 12:5)
- Being understanding (1 Pet. 3:8)
- Being kind (Eph. 4:32)
- Being tolerant (Col. 3:13)
- Giving honor (Rom. 12:10)
- Making peace (Rom. 14:19)
- Giving encouragement (1 Thess. 5:11)
- Expressing Christian love (1 John 3:11)
- Offering guidance (Heb. 3:13)

e. Learning

The local church is a place where Christians not only meet to praise God but also learn more about Him. It is a learning center. Wherever the leaders of the Early Church went, they taught—and Christians learned: "Paul and Barnabas remained in Antioch, where they and many others taught and preached the word of the Lord" (Acts 15:35).

The church's program of Christian education will help you and your family to understand the Bible and ways to apply its truths to your daily living. There will be many opportunities, including Sunday School classes and small-group Bible studies.

The sermon delivered by the pastor or a layperson during the worship service is not just for *inspiration* but also for *edification*—to edify, to build you up in faith. There are some ways you can get the most out of the sermon time:

- Following along in your Bible
- Taking notes, filling out a sermon outline sheet
- Asking God how you should respond to the truths presented
- Reviewing your notes during your private worship times
- Asking questions of other Christians regarding some sermon topic

Public worship has much to offer the disciple of Jesus Christ. But primary to all of its opportunities and activities, the best you will *get out of it* will be linked to what you *put into it*. As you wholeheartedly contribute positively and openly to the parts of that worship—and keep focused on Jesus Christ, not on the wrong attitudes or actions of others—it will be an experience that brings wholeness to your entire week.

④ OBSERVING THE SACRAMENTS

People in Old Testament times used ceremonies as reminders of important spiritual journeys and events. For example, after Joshua led the Israelites across the Jordan River into the land God promised them, God instructed:

> "Choose twelve men from among the people, one from each tribe, and tell them to take up twelve stones from the middle of the Jordan from right where the priests stood and to carry them over with you and put them down at the place where you stay tonight."

> So Joshua called together the twelve men he had appointed from the Israelites, one from each tribe, and said to them, "Go over before the ark of the LORD your God into the middle of the Jordan. Each of you is to take up a stone on his shoulder, according to the number of the tribes of the Israelites, to serve as a sign among you. In the future, when your children ask you, 'What do these stones mean?' tell them that the flow of the Jordan was cut off before the ark of the covenant of the LORD. When it crossed the Jordan, the waters of the Jordan were cut off. These stones are to be a memorial to the people of Israel forever" *(Josh. 4:2-7).*

Sacraments are ceremonies, instituted by Christ, to remind His followers of important moments in their own spiritual journey. The dictionary defines "sacrament" as a "Christian rite . . . that is held to be a means of divine grace or to be a sign or symbol of a spiritual reality."[5] Christ asked His disciples to remember two important events in His life: His baptism and the Lord's Supper (also known as the Eucharist, meaning thanksgiving).

The first, His baptism, was the occasion when His Heavenly Father announced His approval of the life and mission of Jesus, His only Son, prior to the start of His earthly ministry: "As soon as Jesus was baptized, he went up out of the water. At that moment heaven was opened, and he saw the Spirit of God descending like a dove and lighting on him. And a voice from heaven said, 'This is my Son, whom I love; with him I am well pleased'" (Matt. 3:16-17). Jesus' baptism was not a "believer's baptism." Jesus was sinless, so for Him, baptism was not a sign of forgiveness or newness of life; it was rather an example of obedience to His Heavenly Father's assignment for Him. And it was an opportunity for the Heavenly Father to announce that He was the Chosen One.

The second occasion that Christ asks Christians to remember is the Lord's Supper—the time when He had a meal with His disciples just prior to His crucifixion. During that meal He revealed to them the events of His death and its importance to His followers. "While they were eating, Jesus took bread, gave thanks and broke it, and gave it to his disciples, saying, 'Take and eat; this is my body.' Then he took the cup, gave thanks and offered it to them, saying, 'Drink from it, all of you. This is my blood of the covenant, which is poured out for many for the forgiveness of sins'" (Matt. 26:26-28). He instructed His disciples to offer bread and wine as a remembrance of His sacrificial death—the bread representing His body and the wine His blood.

Most Christians observe these two sacraments, baptism and the Lord's Supper, during public worship services on a regular basis. Notice their importance in the faith journey of a disciple of Jesus Christ.

1. BAPTISM

Water baptism is observed by most Christian churches in one of three ways: sprinkling (water is sprinkled onto the head of the baptismal candidate), pouring (water is cupped in the hands of the presiding minister and poured onto the head of the candidate), and immersion (the candidate is dipped into a pool, baptismal tank, or body of water by the presiding minister). Baptism by immersion is usually preferred.

a. The importance of baptism

Jesus referred to baptism as an identifying mark of discipleship. "Whoever believes and is baptized will be saved, but whoever does not believe will be condemned" (Mark 16:16). Jesus also included the observance of baptism in His commission to the disciples to spread the good news of the Kingdom: "Therefore go and make disciples of all nations, baptizing them in the name of the Father and of the Son and of the Holy Spirit" (Matt. 28:19). Just as the ceremonial washings in the Old Testament symbolized cleansing of sin, so also did baptism in the New Testament.

b. The purpose of baptism

Baptism by immersion symbolizes the death (into the water) and resurrection (out of the water) of Jesus Christ—and the candidate's identifying with them. Baptism also signifies the candidate's "death" to the old life of rebellion against God and "life" to the new one of obedience and faith in Christ, "having been buried with him in baptism and raised with him through your faith in the power of God" (Col. 2:12). The ceremony of baptism does not make you a child of God. You are a child of God through faith in the Lord Jesus Christ. Baptism is a sign of that commitment to Christ.

c. The witness of baptism

Baptism not only affirms the candidate's relationship with God through faith in Jesus Christ but also testifies to others about that relationship. The ceremony of baptism is usually witnessed by friends and family in a public worship time. In the New Testament, there are examples of the witness of baptism:

- New converts on the Day of Pentecost (Acts 2:38, 41)
- Samaritan converts (Acts 8:12)
- The Ethiopian eunuch (Acts 8:36)
- Saul (later known as Paul) (Acts 9:18)
- Corinthian Christians (Acts 18:8)
- Ephesian Christians (Acts 19:5)

2. THE LORD'S SUPPER

Observing the Lord's Supper (also known as Communion) was a practice of New Testament Christians. Their obedience to the Master in observing the Lord's Supper became a pattern for all Christians. Paul reminded the church:

> For I received from the Lord what I also passed on to you: The Lord Jesus, on the night he was betrayed, took bread, and when he had given thanks, he broke it and said, "This is my body, which is for you; do this in remembrance of me." In the same way, after supper he took the cup, saying, "This cup is the new covenant in my blood; do this, whenever you drink it, in remembrance of me." For whenever you eat this bread and drink this cup, you proclaim the Lord's death until he comes (1 Cor. 11:23-26).

a. The elements

The elements served during the Lord's Supper observance, the bread and wine, symbolize Christ's provision for our salvation. The bread symbolizes the body of Jesus Christ, which was offered and broken on the Cross of Calvary. The wine (substituted with grape juice in most Protestant churches) represents the blood of Christ, which was shed on that Cross. When you observe Communion you are remembering—and giving praise for—the total commitment that Jesus Christ made for your salvation.

Some denominations say that the elements become the "actual" body and blood of Christ as the participants receive them. Protestant Christianity believes they are only "symbols" of the body and blood of Christ. The sacraments are called means of grace; that is, God uses them to communicate His presence and His blessings. "Communion" also suggests "communication," so observing the Lord's Supper is a time of communication between God and you—and between others and you.

b. Preparing for the Lord's Supper

Some local churches practice "closed Communion," which means that the Communion service is reserved for members of that local church only. Most churches practice "open Communion," which means sharing in the Lord's Supper is open to all believers. "Believers" is the key. It is possible to observe Communion in an "unworthy" manner. The Bible says:

> Whoever eats the bread or drinks the cup of the Lord in an unworthy manner will be guilty of sinning against the body and blood of the Lord. A man ought to examine himself before he eats of the bread and drinks of the cup. For anyone who eats and drinks without recognizing the body of the Lord eats and drinks judgment on himself *(1 Cor. 11:27-29).*

(1) **Those who observe Communion should do so in faith.** Someone who isn't a disciple of Jesus Christ may receive the elements, but that person wouldn't know their true meaning. Participating in the Lord's Supper is an act that testifies of our complete trust in the sacrifice of Christ and that He is the only hope for salvation from being lost: "Salvation is found in no one else, for there is no other name under heaven given to men by which we must be saved" (Acts 4:12).

(2) **Those who observe Communion should do so in harmony with God.** Any unconfessed sin should be repented of. A heart right with God is a heart ready to worship God: "Who may stand in his holy place? He who has clean hands and a pure heart" (Ps. 24:3-4).

(3) **Those who observe Communion should do so in harmony with others.** Paul warned if there was discord with others, it would be detrimental. Christ died to give us a holy relationship with God and spiritual unity with other believers. A forgiving spirit is a prerequisite for the Christian. Jesus said, "Therefore, if you are offering your gift at the altar and there remember that your brother has something against you, leave your gift there in front of the altar. First go and be reconciled to your brother; then come and offer your gift" (Matt. 5:23-24).

Observing the sacraments can be a time of spiritual renewal and Christian fellowship. As you observe them, pray for God's presence, be open and honest to Him, and reach out to others in a spirit of Christian love.

⑤ WITNESSING

Witnessing is in the "job description" of every follower of Jesus Christ. Jesus said, "This is what is written: The Christ will suffer and rise from the dead on the third day, and repentance and forgiveness of sins will be preached in his name to all nations, beginning at Jerusalem. You are witnesses of these things" (Luke 24:46-48).

The news is too good to keep to yourself: "For God so loved the world that he gave his one and only Son, that whoever believes in him shall not perish but have eternal life" (John 3:16). You will want the whole world to know. And that is exactly what the Lord Jesus wants you to do: "All authority in heaven and on earth has been given to me. Therefore go and make disciples of all nations, baptizing them in the name of the Father and of the Son and of the Holy Spirit, and teaching them to obey everything I have commanded you. And surely I am with you always, to the very end of the age" (Matt. 28:18-20).

1. WITNESSING PRINCIPLES

In simplest terms, witnessing is sharing your faith. You tell others what Jesus did for you. In speech, on the printed page, or online, you give a personal account of the commitment you made when you asked the Lord into your life. There are several important principles in Matt. 28 that may be applied to your witnessing:

a. You have the greatest credentials

Jesus said, "All authority in heaven and on earth has been given to me. Therefore go . . ." The word "therefore" makes all the difference. You don't witness in the authority of your name; you witness in the authority of the name of the Lord Jesus Christ. Those are your credentials—His authority is your spiritual passport. You have a spiritual right to tell everyone you meet about God's love and forgiveness through faith in Christ. Witnessing is giving a firsthand account of your life-changing relationship with God. This is seen in the life of one of Jesus' first disciples, "Andrew, Simon Peter's brother, was one of the two who . . . had followed Jesus. The first thing Andrew did was to find his brother Simon and tell him, 'We have found the Messiah' (that is, the Christ). And he brought him to Jesus" (John 1:40-42*a*).

b. You have the greatest assignment

"Make disciples of all nations, baptizing them in the name of the Father and of the Son and of the Holy Spirit." Imagine it, God trusts you to be a part of making a positive influence throughout the earth! You are on God's winning team. The game plan: influencing one person at a time with the gospel (the good news of God's love and forgiveness). You are called to "duplicate your discipleship" in the life of others, who in turn are called to duplicate *their* discipleship—and on and on.

c. You have the greatest promise

"I am with you always, to the very end of the age." Even if you are the only one on your street, on your job, or in your home who is talking about Jesus, you are never alone. Jesus promised He would be there with you, and He shares not only His presence but also His power.

2. WITNESSING PLANS

If you are wondering where to put witnessing principles into practice, the New Testament Book of Acts will give you the best advice. After He had been crucified and had risen from the dead—and prior to His ascension into heaven—Jesus gave His last earthly instructions to the disciples. It was the plan for evangelizing the world: "You will receive power when the Holy Spirit comes on you; and you will be my witnesses in Jerusalem, and in all Judea and Samaria, and to the ends of the earth" (Acts 1:8). The power would come from His Holy Spirit—the third person of the Trinity (God the Father, God the Son, and God the Holy Spirit [cf. Matt. 28:18])—who was revealed on the Day of Pentecost (Acts 2). It was all-inclusive: Jerusalem, Judea, Samaria, and the ends of the earth. Each of the areas mentioned are places where you can be a witness. Let's look closer.

a. "Jerusalem": local

For the disciples, Jerusalem was home base. It was their community. Jesus instructed them to begin their witnessing at home. It's the same for you. Your first "mission field" is in your own community. It may be in your home—to family members. It may be in your local church. It may be on the job (being careful not to use company time). It may be in your local school. The first to know about your new relationship with God through faith in the Lord Jesus Christ are those who are the closest to you. You may ask, "Where do I start?"

(1) Start with your testimony. The media is filled with messages—called testimonials—that endorse a certain product. Some of the testimonials are given spontaneously, but most are rehearsed. Here's a simple plan for advertising the best "product":

(a) What my life was like before Jesus Christ

(b) How I came to know Him

(c) How my life has changed since He is in it

Write it out. Practice it. If you can share from that simple outline in one to three minutes, you are on your way! People want a living example of faith. They need *you* to show them how important it is to have a right relationship with God. There are times when you may need to read your testimony word-for-word, but for the most part, you will want to give it from memory. It shouldn't sound like a canned speech but rather a talk from the heart. In conversational tones, and with honest feeling, present others with an opportunity to decide for Christ.

(2) Learn a presentation plan. Clear directions are always important, and especially clear directions are necessary to tell people how to get to heaven. Learning a simple presentation of the steps to a right relationship with God through faith in the Lord Jesus Christ is a way of giving clear directions. You will find such a plan in your Bible. You may want to write it out and include it on a note or on the cover of your Bible.

- *Admit that you have sinned.* "For all have sinned and fall short of the glory of God" (Rom. 3:23). Explain that disobeying God's known laws is called sin and that sin separates us from God. It also keeps us from enjoying an abundant and purposeful life that God has intended for us.

- *Believe that Jesus Christ died for you.* "Yet to all who received him, to those who believed in his name, he gave the right to become children of God" (John 1:12). Explain that according to the Bible, those who sin die spiritually. But God provided a way for us to be born again spiritually. Jesus Christ paid the penalty of death for us.

- *Confess that Jesus Christ is Lord of your life.* "If you confess with your mouth, 'Jesus is Lord,'

29

and believe in your heart that God raised him from the dead, you will be saved. For it is with your heart that you believe and are justified, and it is with your mouth that you confess and are saved" (Rom. 10:9-10). Explain that "confess" means to "agree with." Explain that we must agree with God that the only way we can be forgiven of our sin is to admit it, to be sorry enough to quit sinning, and to receive Jesus Christ into our hearts by faith, to take the control of our life.

After you have shared your "gospel plan" with someone, you may want to ask if he or she would like to pray a simple prayer to invite Jesus Christ into his or her heart and become His follower. You may want to lead in a prayer and ask the person to repeat it after you. The prayer can be something like this:

Dear Lord Jesus, I know that I am a sinner. I believe that You died for my sins and arose from the grave. I now turn from my sins and invite You to come into my heart and life. I receive You as my personal Savior and follow You as my Lord. Amen.

(3) Gather resource materials. You've probably seen presentations by salespersons, seminar leaders, or teachers that include visuals. As a witness, you might have your own visuals; support material helps to reinforce the message and supply immediate follow-up resources.

(a) Bible. Obviously you won't want to take a giant family Bible with you when you share the gospel—unless it is the only Bible you have. But you will want to have a Bible (a complete Bible or a New Testament). The Bible is the Word of God. You are not just sharing your words; you're sharing God's Word that has been implanted in your heart. Mark the verses in your Bible that outline the gospel presentation plan.

Also, ask your pastor or group leader to give you some follow-up verses from the Bible. Following up a new disciple (one that has prayed the salvation prayer with you) is the first step in helping him or her on the new journey of faith.

(b) Literature. Attractive, four-color (if possible) tracts (printed presentations of the gospel) not only give you another way to share your faith with someone (at a time that would be more convenient for him or her) but also will be an immediate follow-up resource.

(c) Books or booklets. It is important to help the new disciple understand that reading Christian literature is important to spiritual growth. Ask your pastor or group leader to recommend a good book or booklet to share with those with whom you witness.

A book or booklet that has a story of someone's spiritual journey—from being saved to pursuing holiness—might be just the resource to cause someone to invite Christ into his or her life or to see ways to grow in his or her faith.

Here are some other "Jerusalem" (local) opportunities:
- Starting a Bible study group in your neighborhood
- Volunteering in a community ministry
- Offering to give your testimony in a public worship service
- Offering to assist the pastoral team of your church in canvassing a neighborhood to find those interested in knowing more about Christ
- Starting a blog that gives details on your spiritual journey (and ways that people can invite Christ into their lives)
- Participating or coaching in a community sports ministry

b. "Judea": regional

Remember, Christ also asked you to take the gospel beyond your own community. There are neighboring communities—and even surrounding regions—where you may either establish your own ministry or participate in one already established by your church. Those opportunities may include

- Volunteering to be a sponsor or counselor in a camping ministry
- Joining (or forming) a music ministry or drama group for itinerant ministries
- Assisting with the planting of a new church
- Volunteering to help in a compassionate relief effort
- Sponsoring a local or regional church ministry

c. "Ends of the earth": global

Followers of Jesus Christ are called to a global mission. The gospel was not intended for any one people group. It was intended for all.

Jesus said, "This gospel of the kingdom will be preached in the whole world as a testimony to all nations" (Matt. 24:14). You are an important part of that global strategy:

- Pray for missions and missionaries.
- Give toward missions interests.
- Sign up for an overseas missions trip if possible.
- Communicate encouragement to missionaries.
- Learn about mission fields and missionaries.
- Help others understand the importance of missions.

Being one of Christ's disciples is an exciting adventure! Just think, there are *millions* who are waiting to hear what you have heard; and millions who will respond in the way you responded.

⑥ DISCIPLING OTHER BELIEVERS

Discipling is the sixth "discipline" of a disciple. You have already heard the Great Commission of Jesus Christ: "Go and make disciples . . ." (Matt. 28:19), and you have heard that discipling is building up other believers in their faith, now let's talk about strategy.

The highest level of discipling was that of Christ's. In three short years of earthly ministry, He not only preached before and taught multitudes of people but also led an ongoing small-group study. He equipped 12 men, called the 12 apostles, to carry out a global ministry that turned their world upside down. They were His disciples (Matt. 10:2-4).

In studying the ministry of Jesus to His apostles we see insights into the discipling process.

1. HE PRAYED FOR THEM

To one apostle He said, "I have prayed for you, Simon, that your faith may not fail. And when you have turned back, strengthen your brothers" (Luke 22:32). He knew how the devil would try to destroy the apostles' faith in Him. He knew that the busyness of life would often distract them. He knew there would be temptations to go with the crowd instead of standing alone for the right. So He prayed.

As God gives you opportunity to disciple new believers, begin that assignment with prayer. Put them on your prayer list. Pray every day:

- Pray that they will read and study God's Word.
- Pray that the Holy Spirit will empower them to live for Christ.
- Pray that family members or associates will see a change in them.
- Pray that they will be faithful in attending a local church.
- Pray that the enemy will not have power over their decision making.
- Pray that they will find a place of service for the Lord.
- Pray that they will be delivered from addictive behavior.
- Pray that they will grow in their faith.

They will depend not only on your advice but also on your prayers. Be faithful in meeting *with* them. But also be faithful in meeting God *about* them.

2. HE MINISTERED TO THEM

Jesus taught the greatest truths in the simplest way. That is seen in Jesus' recruiting the apostles: "As Jesus was walking beside the Sea of Galilee, he saw two brothers, Simon called Peter and his brother Andrew. They were casting a net into the lake, for they were fishermen. 'Come, follow me,' Jesus said, 'and I will make you fishers of men.' At once they left their nets and followed him" (Matt. 4:18-20). They may not have understood world evangelization, but they knew fishing. Jesus met them where they were.

Just as you learned—and continue to learn—more about the Bible, those whom you disciple will need to learn. They may not be acquainted with Bible reading, or even with the Bible. They may need to know very basic beliefs. Your patience in teaching them at their level of understanding will be of great value.

3. HE ENCOURAGED THEM

When Jesus sent His apostles to minister, He didn't paint a rosy picture, "All men will hate you because of me, but he who stands firm to the end will be saved. When you are persecuted in one place, flee to another. I tell you the truth, you will not finish going through the cities of Israel before the Son of Man comes" (Matt. 10:22-23). He didn't hide the hardships, but He gave them hope as well.

Those you disciple may have a rather naive idea of what it is like to serve the Lord. You won't want to rain on their parade, but you will also need to warn them that being a Christian includes adversity as well as adventure. The devil will stalk them (1 Pet. 5:8), and others will talk about them. Yet they must know that they are on the winning side; they must know that Jesus forever won the victory for them on the Cross (John 19:30).

- Lead them to the promises of God's Word.
- Lead them to the prophecies of God's Word.
- Lead them to the priorities of God's Word.

4. HE SPENT TIME WITH THEM

"The apostles gathered around Jesus and reported to him all they had done and taught. Then, because so many people were coming and going that they did not even have a chance to eat, he said to them, 'Come with me by yourselves to a quiet place and get some rest.' So they went away by themselves in a boat to a solitary place" (Mark 6:30-32). Jesus wanted them to know that discipleship wasn't all about work. They needed times of relaxation. And those times of relaxation were times when He could fellowship with them.

Make time for the person you are discipling:
- Include some relaxation times as well as study times.
- Take them with you to a concert or seminar.
- Enjoy the fellowship of having a cup of coffee.
- Learn to know them as persons—and let them know you.

5. HE TAUGHT THEM

Some of the best teachings the apostles received were on the job. Situations would arise that gave Jesus an opportunity to apply spiritual truth to the incident. It happened when Jesus was planning to feed the thousands who had come to hear Him speak: "The disciples had forgotten to bring bread, except for one loaf they had with them in the boat. 'Be careful,' Jesus warned them. 'Watch out for the yeast of the Pharisees and that of Herod'" (Mark 8:14-15). The lesson included the danger of neglect. He taught them that spiritual preparation included watching out for the false teachers around them.

Your discipleship will not just be focused on a study but also will include lessons from life. Use those opportunities that arise to make spiritual applications. For example, a death in the community may be a good time to talk about being certain of salvation or the hope of the resurrection. You might also want the person you disciple to share his or her experiences of the day or the week. Those experiences will be links to some biblical truth.

33

6. HE CORRECTED THEM

There will be times when you will have to correct your disciple about attitudes or actions that are contrary to God's Word. Jesus corrected His disciples:

Then he got into the boat and his disciples followed him. Without warning, a furious storm came up on the lake, so that the waves swept over the boat. But Jesus was sleeping. The disciples went and woke him, saying, "Lord, save us! We're going to drown!" He replied, "You of little faith, why are you so afraid?" Then he got up and rebuked the winds and the waves, and it was completely calm *(Matt. 8:23-26).*

Those whom you disciple are living in a hostile world. It will be easy for them to copy the behavior of the worldly, including its doubts. It will be your job to lovingly and carefully point out the difference between a worldview and a Christ-view. Leading questions may be used to bring the disciples back "on track." For example, you may ask them how a certain attitude or action squares with God's Word. Respect is earned. You will need to show the disciples that

- You believe in them.
- You are praying for them.
- You don't have all the answers.

7. HE DEFENDED THEM

As the greatest leader, Jesus often came to the defense of His followers. In one instance He both defended the actions of His apostles and foretold His resurrection:

> Some people came and asked Jesus, "How is it that John's disciples and the disciples of the Pharisees are fasting, but yours are not?" Jesus answered, "How can the guests of the bridegroom fast while he is with them? They cannot, so long as they have him with them. But the time will come when the bridegroom will be taken from them, and on that day they will fast" *(Mark 2:18-20).*

Not only are you your disciples' teacher, but you are also their defender. Following Christ often involves a break with former associates. Your disciples will probably experience misunderstanding by some and outright ridicule by others. On top of that, the enemy of their faith, Satan, will constantly accuse them of not measuring up (Rev. 12:10). Let those you disciple know that you will stand by them—even when others may stand against them. That will also include spiritual warfare with Satan (Eph. 6:12).

- Send them an encouraging e-mail or note.
- Call them when you hear of difficult times in their lives.
- Constantly remind them of your availability and interest.
- Share some promises from the Bible.

8. HE CHALLENGED THEM

Some who make the greatest spiritual impact are those who face the greatest challenges. The challenges actually put a fire in their hearts. Jesus didn't call His apostles to a life of ease; He called them to a life of challenge:

> Calling the Twelve to him, he sent them out two by two and gave them authority over evil spirits. These were his instructions: "Take nothing for the journey except a staff—no bread, no bag, no money in your belts. Wear sandals but not an extra tunic. Whenever you enter a house, stay there until you leave that town. And if any place will not welcome you or listen to you, shake the dust off your feet when you leave, as a testimony against them" *(Mark 6:7-11).*

They would have to depend on God, not on their own efforts. The Holy Spirit would need to empower them against their adversaries.

Don't be afraid to challenge your disciples. Set some goals and objectives. For example, assign a Bible reading or a prayer time. Follow up with them to let them know you were serious about the assignment. Set some evangelism goals. Draw up a prayer list of their friends or associates who need to know Christ as Savior and then commit to praying for those same people. When people aren't challenged, they often become lazy or indifferent.

9. HE TRUSTED THEM

Jesus gave the greatest work of all to 12 people who didn't have any previous experience. So He called them and trained them, assigned and encouraged them, and He sent them and inquired of them. As Matt. 10:1 recounts, "He called his twelve disciples to him and gave them authority to drive out evil spirits and to heal every disease and sickness."

He knew how faithful they would need to be. He knew how courageous they would need to be. He knew how lonely they would be. Yet He assigned them to do battle with hell itself. He trusted them.

Let those you disciple know that you trust them. Let them know you
- Trust their decision making
- Trust their dependence upon God
- Trust their vision to reach others for Christ
- Trust their commitment of faith

Like an infant, they will have to learn to walk. They will make mistakes. They may hurt or be hurt. They won't do things the "right" way. But they will need to know that you believe in them, that you trust their walk with the Lord.

"Go and make disciples . . ." Christ's call is as fresh today as it was when He first spoke those words. Listen for His leading. Look for someone you can pour your life into. And watch as a new believer grows in faith and knowledge.

⑦ STEWARDSHIP

The Bible says, "It is required in stewards that one be found faithful" (1 Cor. 4:2, NKJV). The wise and disciplined use of God's resources in your personal life is highly important. In fact, in one of Jesus' parables (stories from life that teach spiritual truth), He implies that He will be in charge of the audit. Jesus taught His disciples: "There was a rich man whose manager was accused of wasting his possessions. So he called him in and asked him, 'What is this I hear about you? Give an account of your management'" (Luke 16:1-2).

A steward manages the assets of another. As we have mentioned, God is not only the Creator of the world but also the Owner. Again, Ps. 24:1 says, "The earth is the LORD's, and everything in it." He has the sovereign rights over every earthly asset.

When you acknowledge His ownership and His rights, and determine to carefully manage those assets, you have taken the first step of Christian stewardship. Stewardship involves the wise use of our time, our talent, and our treasure.

Every biblical teaching about being a steward ends with giving an account. We will have to give an answer for the way we used God's resources, whether in the care of the planet or in the care of a checking account. God's requirements for giving are in proportion to His gifts to us. And we do have indebtedness. He created us. He gave us biblical principles so that we might live in health and safety. He died on the Cross for us. He provides food, shelter, transportation, sunshine, rivers, and so forth. There is no end to what God has given to us. So our stewardship of His gifts gives honor and thanksgiving to Him.

Notice some important areas of stewardship:

1. TIME

Every person on earth starts the day with the same amount of minutes and hours. In that regard, everyone is equal. But not everyone uses the minutes and hours of the day in a wise and disciplined way. That's why the New Testament writer said, "Be very careful, then, how you live—not as unwise but as wise, making the most of every opportunity, because the days are evil" (Eph. 5:15-16).

Because of sin's influence, the opportunity to use time for selfish and worldly endeavors will always be present. Christians are called to "redeem" the time—to reclaim it and to put it to use for the pursuit of holiness, personally and in the faith community. Many nonfaith pursuits can lead to emotional and spiritual turmoil—including anxiety, broken relationships, and financial ruin.

There are ways to give honor and thanksgiving to God in giving back a portion of your time to Him:

- Volunteer time in the local church ministry.
- Volunteer time in a church-related organization.
- Spend a certain amount of time each day in showing kindness and concern to others (e-mail, phone call, note, letter, help, etc.).
- Have a daily prayer time, bringing the concerns of church leaders, national leaders, and community leaders before God.

- Visit those who are hospitalized or imprisoned, sharing the gospel or giving encouragement.
- Lead a small-group Bible study.
- Teach a Sunday School class.
- Take part in a community outreach event.

The list could go on and on. Each day, God freely gives you 24 brand-new hours. Christian stewardship involves giving a portion of those hours back to Him in thankfulness and in obedience to His Word.

2. TALENT

Remember, each person is given an ability that can be used to glorify God: "There are different kinds of gifts, but the same Spirit. There are different kinds of service, but the same Lord. There are different kinds of working, but the same God works all of them in all men. Now to each one the manifestation of the Spirit is given for the common good" (1 Cor. 12:4-7).

You may wish you could play keyboards or sing like the musicians on the platform or stage. You might even be able to do those things, but if not, you have some other gift that can be used in service to the Lord. You are practicing stewardship when you use your talent in supporting and building God's kingdom. Beside music or speaking, each local church has a variety of tasks that call for a variety of talents. To name a few:

- Cooking
- Serving
- Building maintaining
- Vehicle maintaining
- Equipment maintaining
- Landscaping
- Remodeling
- Contracting
- Planning
- Driving
- Telephoning
- Mailing
- Cleaning
- Painting
- Writing
- Designing
- Publishing
- Computer networking
- Lighting
- Sewing
- Fund-raising
- Woodworking
- Visiting
- Canvassing
- Accounting
- Ushering

- Greeting
- Hosting
- Baby-sitting
- Training
- Advertising
- Marketing
- Plumbing
- Installing
- Heating and cooling
- Acting
- Inspecting
- Filing
- Counseling
- Praying

There is something for you to do. Sharing your talent is a way to express your faithfulness to the Lord Jesus Christ—in His church.

3. TREASURE

As we have noticed, God has established a standard for Christian giving. It's called a "tithe." Tithe means "tenth." Malachi 3:10 says, "'Bring the whole tithe into the storehouse, that there may be food in my house. Test me in this,' says the LORD Almighty, 'and see if I will not throw open the floodgates of heaven and pour out so much blessing that you will not have room enough for it.'" In Old Testament times, the "storehouse" was an added room where worshippers brought a portion of their crops as a "tithe" to support worship in the Temple. To us, the storehouse is the local church.

Jesus taught the practice of giving the "tenth" in New Testament times: "Woe to you, teachers of the law and Pharisees, you hypocrites! You give a tenth of your spices—mint, dill and cumin. But you have neglected the more important matters of the law—justice, mercy and faithfulness. You should have practiced the latter, *without neglecting the former*" (Matt. 23:23, emphasis added). Generosity was never a substitute for righteousness. Both principles were to be obeyed—then and now.

Tithing (giving a tenth) is the fairest standard for giving possible. The person who earned little is instructed to give the same percentage as the person who earned more. And both were given the same promise: "See if I will not throw open the floodgates of heaven and pour out so much blessing that you will not have room enough for it." In essence, God has promised to bless the giving of the tithe—and the tither!

The giving of our treasure to the Lord is just as important as the giving of our time and talents. For the growing Christian, tithing is not a duty; it is a delight (Ps. 40:8). God also delights in our obedience in giving: "Each man should give what he has decided in his heart to give, not reluctantly or under compulsion, for God loves a cheerful giver" (2 Cor. 9:7).

You can start tithing by putting aside a tenth of your income and giving it through the local church. You would also be wise to put aside 10 percent of your income for savings. You'll be surprised how far the other 80 percent will go! God brings the increase. He promised it, and He always keeps His promise.

But for disciples who are serious about their spiritual journey, giving a tithe is just the beginning. They may want to give an offering above their tithe. One thing they will soon learn: You can never outgive God!

⑧ CHURCH MEMBERSHIP

When you became a follower of Jesus Christ, you became a part of the family of God (John 1:12). Commitment to an organized unit of that family (the local church)—including identifying with its core beliefs, participating in its ministries, and cooperating in its leadership—is a disciplined step. You can attend any local church without being a member of its organization, but there are real advantages to membership.

1. CHURCH MEMBERSHIP IS AN OPPORTUNITY TO DEFEND THE CHURCH

The Church (all believers in Christ) is under attack by its enemies. There are those who seek to destroy it from without. For example, some nations have made it a crime to be a part of the organized church. By joining a local church you are defending its rightful place in society. The organized church has been on the front lines of the greatest battles for the reforms of society—social, judicial, racial, and educational. It still wages some of those battles. By joining a church rather than just attending, you publicly align yourself with its struggle to better the world.

There are those who would seek to destroy it from within. The spiritual attacks of the enemy, Satan, have caused its leaders to make wrong priorities. Instead of obeying its original marching orders to preach the gospel in all the world, the church, in some places, has turned its attention to meeting its own needs. Being a Christ-centered, Christ-directed member of the church is an opportunity to help keep it on course. Your voice and your vote are like a rudder on a ship that moves it in the direction that the Captain commands. "Christ loved the church and gave himself up for her to make her holy, cleansing her by the washing with water through the word, and to present her to himself as a radiant church, without stain or wrinkle or any other blemish, but holy and blameless" (Eph. 5:25-27).

2. CHURCH MEMBERSHIP IS AN OPPORTUNITY TO ALIGN WITH THE CHURCH'S BELIEFS

The apostle Peter warned, "First of all, you must understand that in the last days scoffers will come, scoffing and following their own evil desires" (2 Pet. 3:3). It could be said that this is an age of doubting and unbelief—an age without definite moral and religious stands. The "anything goes" trend in the world is negatively affecting almost every segment of society. Someone once said if you don't stand for something, you will fall for anything. The local church stands for something. The local church is founded on biblical beliefs (doctrines) of the Bible. By joining with it, you help to defend its core values.

With the preparation most churches ask of membership candidates (usually taking membership classes), you will learn more about its biblical beliefs. You will be enriched to know the importance and relevance of God's Word.

3. CHURCH MEMBERSHIP IS AN OPPORTUNITY TO DEVELOP LEADERSHIP SKILLS

In most churches leadership is restricted to their members. Joining the local church will give you an opportunity to develop or strengthen your leadership skills. For example, becoming a departmental leader in the Sunday School demands many of the same skills used in supervising people in the workforce.

Churches also offer leadership training. That training not only could help you in church ministry but also could make you more effective in other areas of life. A class on child behavior, for instance, could give you insights into developing parenting skills. Church membership usually opens wider doors of opportunity than just attending a church. For one thing, membership introduces you to the largest—and usually the most loyal—leadership segment of the local church. You will gain skills by interacting with them in a leader-led ministry of the church. That principle characterized the Early Church: "They devoted themselves to the apostles' teaching and to the fellowship, to the breaking of bread and to prayer" (Acts 2:42).

4. CHURCH MEMBERSHIP IS AN OPPORTUNITY TO ADD STRENGTH TO THE CHURCH'S OUTREACH

The local church's mission is to reach unbelievers with the gospel of Jesus Christ, lead them into a relationship with Jesus Christ, and then build them up in the faith. It also has a mandate to plant other churches. You can be a part of that exciting effort. In fact, you may be the very person who will add strength to that effort. You have a network of friends, family members, and associates that can be influenced by the local church.

As a member, you will likely be more involved in the church's outreach than if you were just an attendee.

- The burden of the church becomes your burden.
- The cause of the church becomes your cause.
- The priorities of the church become your priorities.

5. CHURCH MEMBERSHIP IS AN OPPORTUNITY TO HAVE A VOICE IN THE CHURCH'S DIRECTION

In most churches the church's major moves are decided by its membership. You may cast a vote on a certain issue that will affect the future of your church. Your input could be one that will help the local church decide on a biblical purpose. Your enthusiasm for growth could be contagious. The church may reach new heights by catching your vision.

Of course, the church is made up of human beings, and human beings are not always mission-oriented or purpose-driven. In many cases they will make decisions based on comfort or convenience. But in other cases they may need a role model. The apostle Paul instructed a young pastor named Timothy, "Don't let anyone look down on you because you are young, but set an example for the believers in speech, in life, in love, in faith and in purity" (1 Tim. 4:12).

The very church that you are considering joining came about because someone had a vision to start it. Someone refused the status quo and launched the very movement that resulted in your church. You could be that someone for some church in the future.

6. CHURCH MEMBERSHIP IS AN OPPORTUNITY TO HELP DETERMINE A CHURCH'S LEADERSHIP

Many local churches rise or fall based on their leadership. A church's pastoral staff or its governing board may or may not have a vision for reaching the lost or expanding the kingdom of God. In most of those situations, leadership positions are appointed or approved by the vote of its membership. You have an opportunity to prayerfully influence the purpose and mission of the local church's leadership team. In the Early Church the disciples needed to add to their staff because of its growth. A "nominating committee" of disciples put the names before the governing body: "They presented these men to the apostles, who prayed and laid their hands on them. So the word of God spread. The number of disciples in Jerusalem increased rapidly, and a large number of priests became obedient to the faith" (Acts 6:6-7).

Membership may even result in you becoming a part of that leadership team. You may then be able to work from within the organization to think about its place in the community—and to make appropriate changes to give it great effectiveness.

7. CHURCH MEMBERSHIP IS AN OPPORTUNITY TO INFLUENCE YOUR FAMILY

Church membership has a loyalty factor. Loyalty has changed in philosophy and practice from generation to generation. Twenty-first-century ministry is far different from even 20th-century ministry, for example. Today, people often choose churches in the same way they choose stores in a shopping center. By joining a local church you may have a great opportunity to grow loyalty in your own family. The commitment of just one person can result in the commitment of many. Usually those who make the greatest impact on others have a loyalty to their ideals and institutions. It was probably a loyal church member who

- Invited you to your first church service
- First told you about Jesus
- Introduced you to a supportive Christian friend
- Taught you the importance of Bible reading
- Prayed for your need

8. CHURCH MEMBERSHIP IS AN OPPORTUNITY TO INFLUENCE OTHER BELIEVERS

Many Christians are not loyal to a single church. They go from church to church, seeking a better program, bigger facilities, or different worship styles. Without "church roots," those who are "shoppers" are often unsettled spiritually. Finding a church and joining it is an example to other believers. Friends or associates might see by your membership that being connected to a local church could have a positive effect on their spiritual growth. In fact, you may influence them to join your church.

- Invite them to a church event that would be of interest to them.
- Give them a chance to meet other members during a fellowship time.
- Learn about the ministries of the church that would directly affect them.
- Share information about the church through brochures or its Web site.

9. CHURCH MEMBERSHIP IS AN OPPORTUNITY TO BE A PART OF THE CHURCH'S MINISTRY TEAM

Being linked with the church through membership will give you a better understanding of its different ministries. You will soon discover places within the organization where you can plug in your talents and interests. You will also have an opportunity to learn about people who need your ministry specialty. Membership gives you an inside track on the needs of the congregation. The Early Church is an example: "All the believers were together and had everything in common. Selling their possessions and goods, they gave to anyone as he had need" (Acts 2:44-45).

10. CHURCH MEMBERSHIP IS AN OPPORTUNITY
TO HELP GUIDE THE CHURCH'S STEWARDSHIP DECISIONS

The church organization, as well as its members, should be careful to use God's resources in a way that brings glory to Him. Church membership will likely give you an opportunity to approve or disapprove the church's major expenditures. And membership will likely give you the opportunity to help guide the church's stewardship through the approval of a yearly budget. Also, your financial interest in its ministry will give you the joy of seeing the positive results.

Stability, opportunity, identity—committing to join a local church as a member is one way to help strengthen the influence of the church in the community and, subsequently, in the world.

SECTION TWO

D-I-S-C-I-P-L-E
(Developing a Disciple)

⑨ CASTING THE VISION

A Eurasian team member with the *JESUS* Film Harvest Partners told of a college student who prayed to receive Christ: "At the end of the film showing, we sang a hymn and prayed to the Lord. After the prayer was over a college student . . . stood up and said, 'My heart has been touched by something else. Might this be the Lord Jesus reaching me with His love? I want to respond to Him right now.'"[6] Yes, it was the Lord Jesus reaching with His love. But someone needed to be an extension of His heart and His hands. That's where the film team came in. And that's where you come in. You have an unprecedented opportunity to be the heart and hands of the Savior reaching out to people with the love of Christ.

Evangelism and discipleship is just as important now as it was in the Early Church, and perhaps more. There is an increasing trend to grow churches by "harvesting" from other churches, reflected in percentage points on church reports but not in the bottom-line growth of the church. Real growth is conversion growth: "And the Lord added to their number daily those who were being saved" (Acts 2:47).

Author and missionary Joel Comiskey quoted Tom Clegg and Warren Bird in his article "Truth and Myth About Evangelism and Community: How Small-Group Community and Mission Fit Together": "The fact is that, in America, it takes the combined efforts of eighty-five Christians, working over an entire year to produce one convert. Half of all churches do not add one new person through conversion growth."[7] A new tide of evangelism must sweep across the church. Believers must be equipped with a plan to win people to Christ and then disciple them in their faith.

What happens to that Eurasian college student after he is saved?

- He begins a follow-up Bible study to learn about being Christ's disciple.
- He will have an opportunity to join a small-group Bible study or be part of a church plant.
- Then, prayerfully, the young man's faith will be replicated in the life of another through discipleship training.

Paul's discipleship plan still works: "And the things you have heard me say in the presence of many witnesses entrust to reliable men who will also be qualified to teach others" (2 Tim. 2:2). The wisdom writer said, "Where there is no revelation, the people cast off restraint; but happy is he who keeps the law" (Prov. 29:18, NKJV). The enemy is waging a tenacious campaign to win the souls of men and women and boys and girls. God has placed you on the battle lines. You are called to bring them over to God's side. God wants to give you 20/20 vision for evangelism and discipleship.

1. CATCHING THE VISION

"But where do I start?" you might ask. **First, start on your knees in prayer or in a prayer walk.** Get alone with God and ask Him to enlighten and empower you by His Spirit to reach your Jerusalem, Judea, and Samaria (Acts 1:8). Then allow Him to plant that vision in your heart.

Second, utilize a plan, such as big brothers/big sisters or prayer cells (see Appendix I) for enlisting believers in evangelizing or discipling. But it will take more than principles or plans. It will take a heart—your heart—that is fully yielded to God. Discipleship isn't just about adding people to an earthly organization; it's about increasing the Kingdom. Catch the vision—and then cast it!

Third, perceive it. Think about what God wants to do in your community:

- People won to Christ and filled with the Holy Spirit
- Broken relationships healed
- Believers leading others to Christ and discipling them

- Churches praying and working together in outreach
- Churches born out of your church

A sanctified heart is filled with faith in what God said He will do. A young boy suffering from demon possession was brought by his father to Jesus. The father said of the demon, "Often he has thrown him both into the fire and into the water to destroy him" (Mark 9:22a, NKJV). Then he asked Jesus in a roundabout way if He could help: "But if You can do anything, have compassion on us and help us" (v. 22b, NKJV). Jesus' reaction was one of authority over the man's doubt:

> "If you can believe, all things are possible to him who believes." Immediately the father of the child cried out and said with tears, "Lord, I believe; help my unbelief!" When Jesus saw that the people came running together, He rebuked the unclean spirit, saying to it, "Deaf and dumb spirit, I command you, come out of him and enter him no more!" Then the spirit cried out, convulsed him greatly, and came out of him. And he became as one dead, so that many said, "He is dead." But Jesus took him by the hand and lifted him up, and he arose *(vv. 23-27, NKJV).*

"All things are possible to him who believes." That's God's Word. Perceive it. Open your mind to a new thing. Let God show you the possibilities in times of prayer and confession.

Fourth, plant it. Once the spark of outreach is lit in your heart, let it burn! But let that fire spread: Share the vision with an accountability partner, prayer partner, or board member. Plant the vision enthusiastically in his or her heart.

- Agree together on God's promise (Matt. 18:19).
- If you can't meet together for regular prayer meetings, make a covenant of prayer to pray at the same time each day for God's direction and anointing.
- Pray for revival in your own hearts.
- Confess your needs to the Lord. Make wrongs right—asking forgiveness where necessary.
- Humble your hearts before God and trust Him for an outpouring of His Spirit.

2. CASTING THE VISION

The next step is to widen the influence. Draw in other prayer partners and share the vision with them. Make a similar covenant of prayer. Distribute a prayer list, outlining the general areas of need:

- Outreach vision
- Discipling believers
- Leadership vision
- Campaign plan
- Workers
- Schedule
- Target areas

Now include your extended leadership team. Spend some time during organizational meetings focusing on praying for the outreach of your church. Ask your denominational leaders for recommended resources; schedule laypersons from other churches to give testimonies of revival and outreach; utilize media presentations during worship services to motivate the congregation to think about outreach; post signage that reminds your congregation about the Great Commission.

Authors Bill and Amy Stearns challenge:

> Go ahead: Break out of the Christian-culture idea that to join God's family is to become part of a respectable, privileged group that attends lots of meetings. Being a follower of Je-

sus is more like being born into a bustling family business—a high-risk business with pressures, challenges, dangerous competition as well as profit-sharing, camaraderie, and job satisfaction. When you're born into this family business everybody takes part in the Father's work.[8]

Go ahead and plan it. Acts 16:6-10 says:

> Paul and his companions traveled throughout the region of Phrygia and Galatia, having been kept by the Holy Spirit from preaching the word in the province of Asia. When they came to the border of Mysia, they tried to enter Bithynia, but the Spirit of Jesus would not allow them to. So they passed by Mysia and went down to Troas. During the night Paul had a vision of a man of Macedonia standing and begging him, "Come over to Macedonia and help us." After Paul had seen the vision, we got ready at once to leave for Macedonia, concluding that God had called us to preach the gospel to them.

Notice, "After Paul had seen the vision, we got ready at once . . ." Spirit-led decisions were turned into Spirit-led plans, which became one of the greatest missionary efforts in history.

3. D-I-S-C-I-P-L-E

Discipleship is a disciplined effort to become a more effective follower of Jesus Christ. In Section One we covered eight disciplines that every follower of Christ should practice:

1. Pursuing holiness
2. Private worship
3. Public worship
4. Observing the sacraments
5. Witnessing
6. Discipling other believers
7. Stewardship
8. Church membership

That's the basic—the "minimum daily requirement." Disciplers should not only be familiar with those disciplines but also practice them. In fact, they should take the lead in modeling the disciplines. Again, the best discipleship is "caught." Paul says in 1 Cor. 11:1, "Follow my example, as I follow the example of Christ."

There are eight additional areas of concentration in developing a disciple:

1. Develop an intentional friendship with the disciple.
2. Identify the disciple's spiritual understanding levels.
3. Supply a spiritual support system.
4. Contact the disciple about spiritual progress/needs.
5. Incorporate the disciple into the life/ministries of the church.
6. Pray daily for the disciple's spiritual growth.
7. Look for the disciple's spiritual gifts.
8. Enlist the disciple in ministry.

The acrostic D-I-S-C-I-P-L-E may be used as a reminder to focus on those key areas. Your objective is to develop a "whole" disciple, one that is well-rounded in knowledge and experience in key areas of the Christian faith. How do you accomplish it? D-I-S-C-I-P-L-E.

D—Develop an intentional friendship

Discipleship happens on a personal level—one person develops an intentional, personal, caring relationship with another. In other words, they make a commitment of emotional and spiritual time

47

and energy. The process includes self-sacrificing love. Jesus said, "Your love for one another will prove to the world that you are my disciples" (John 13:35, NLT).

I—Identify spiritual understanding levels

Paul the apostle made an observation about spiritual maturity levels in his letter to early Christians in Corinth: "I gave you milk, not solid food, for you were not yet ready for it" (1 Cor. 3:2). Disciplers work with disciples at their level of spiritual understanding. They recognize that the amount of spiritual truth that disciples process depends on their ability to understand that truth. Granted the Holy Spirit leads us into truth (John 16:13), but that leadership is through divinely given intelligence, reason, and conscience—and you can be a voice of that Spirit-directed leadership.

The apostle John recognized that spiritual understanding levels also vary according to age and experience. In fact, three levels of maturity are identified:

"Newcomers"

"Children"

"Veterans"

First John 2:12-14 (TM) says:

> I remind you, my dear children: Your sins are forgiven in Jesus' name. You veterans were in on the ground floor, and know the One who started all this; you newcomers have won a big victory over the Evil One. And a second reminder, dear children: You know the Father from personal experience. You veterans know the One who started it all; and you newcomers—such vitality and strength! God's word is so steady in you. Your fellowship with God enables you to gain a victory over the Evil One.

Similar stages will soon become evident in the discipling process. You will need to learn how to identify those stages and disciple those persons accordingly.

S—Supply a support system

We are dependent on support systems our whole life. From child care to geriatric care, the supervision of knowledgeable people either tells us how to live or keeps us alive. In one sense a discipler does the same. Your knowledgeable supervision teaches disciples how to live and protects them from harm. Your support system will include

Prayer

Bible study

Fellowship times

Communications of encouragement

Guidance toward ministry

You not only are a partner with them but also are related to them by faith in Jesus Christ. Discipleship is caring for a family member spiritually.

C—Contact regarding spiritual progress/needs

Both modern and standard means of communication will strengthen your spiritual bonding with a disciple. There is a "golden hour" of communication when you can zero in on the needs of your disciple. In a minimum of 60 minutes per week, you can express God's love and affirmation.

I—Incorporate into the life/ministries of the church

Your disciple will need to learn—by your testimony and example—how important the local church is to spiritual growth. From a basic knowledge of the church and its beliefs to the ministries it offers individuals and families, your disciple needs the fellowship of other believers. You will discover ways that will make it easier for the disciple to become involved in the "current" of the church.

P—Pray daily for spiritual growth

Christ's first disciples not only ministered well in their teaching, administrative, and writing skills but also were effective in prayer. You will stand alongside your disciples as they face the enemy himself. Your intercessory prayer will be crucial for their survival against the attacks of the devil and his forces. Learning how to be that effective intercessor is a crucial part of the discipling effort.

L—Look for spiritual gifts

Even before they were spiritually reborn, God has gifted your disciples with abilities and interests that will help build the Kingdom. Your task as a discipler is to

- Learn ways to discern their spiritual gifts.
- Enlighten them about those gifts.
- Encourage them to use them for Christ.

You will also need to teach them about the Holy Spirit's activity in giving spiritual gifts and of His intent to empower those gifts through entire sanctification.

E—Enlist in ministry

You will teach by your example how rewarding ministry can be. You will learn how to encourage your disciples to take part in a local church ministry. Your disciples will learn the importance of not "sitting in the stands." They will learn the importance of being on the "playing field." You will be their coach-encourager.

The greatest ship in a cruise line is merely an aluminum and steel monument of human engineering and ingenuity when it is tied to the dock. Its true splendor is in its moving away from the dock into the open seas. And every part of that movement is dependent on a power source hidden below deck.

Help your disciples chart the course and move away from the dock. Your task is to make the investment of your time and energy in their lives—and let God do the rest. Oswald Chambers said, "To be a disciple means that we deliberately identify ourselves with God's interests in other people."[9] That's it! It's all about people. Jesus died for people. Your ministry isn't just about properties or personnel; it's about people.

- Winning people to Christ
- Discipling believers to become disciples
- Starting Bible studies
- Planting new churches

Catch the vision, and then cast it to others!

⑩ DEVELOP INTENTIONAL RELATIONSHIPS

The dictionary defines "relationship" as "the way two or more people feel and behave towards each other."[10] Relationships, then, involve attitudes and actions of one person toward another. For the disciple, "intentional relationships" are focused attitudes and actions toward others that strengthen interaction and ultimately lead to a greater common knowledge of the Lord Jesus Christ.

Perhaps one of the greatest intentional relationships of the New Testament is modeled in Christ's meeting with Zacchaeus.

> Jesus entered Jericho and was passing through. A man was there by the name of Zacchaeus; he was a chief tax collector and was wealthy. He wanted to see who Jesus was, but being a short man he could not, because of the crowd. So he ran ahead and climbed a sycamore-fig tree to see him, since Jesus was coming that way. When Jesus reached the spot, he looked up and said to him, "Zacchaeus, come down immediately. I must stay at your house today." So he came down at once and welcomed him gladly. All the people saw this and began to mutter, "He has gone to be the guest of a 'sinner.'" But Zacchaeus stood up and said to the Lord, "Look, Lord! Here and now I give half of my possessions to the poor, and if I have cheated anybody out of anything, I will pay back four times the amount." Jesus said to him, "Today salvation has come to this house, because this man, too, is a son of Abraham. For the Son of Man came to seek and to save what was lost" *(Luke 19:1-10).*

This incident gives us important insight into discipling others:

1. LOOK FOR THE INTENTIONAL MOMENT

Notice first that this relationship developed during the daily routine. Jesus "was passing through." The event seems to have just happened. Some of the best discipleship situations just happen. Whether leading someone *to* Christ or building him or her up *in* Christ, discipling events often happen during the daily routine.

But be sure that it was an event born of purpose: "The Son of Man came to seek and to save what was lost" (Luke 19:10). His eyes were peeled for those who needed a way out of the condition they were in. He also advised His disciples to stay alert: "Open your eyes and look at the fields" (John 4:35). Look for the intentional moment.

- An expressed need
- An obvious need
- A serious question
- A Spirit-led opportunity

For every disciple there is a divine "moment." There is a window of opportunity that may never open again. The disciple must be prepared: (1) spiritually, by being familiar with evangelism and discipleship methods; (2) socially, by being willing to work with all people groups; and (3) physically, by having eyes and ears that are open to the cries of the needy.

2. IDENTIFY THE PROSPECT

"When Jesus reached the spot, he looked up and said to him, 'Zacchaeus . . .'" Not only did Jesus know who Zacchaeus was, but He also knew what he needed. Jesus had a heart of compassion that should be characteristic of every disciple (Phil. 2:5). From the moment He saw Zacchaeus, the Master planned to establish an intentional relationship with him.

The prospects for intentional relationships in discipleship may include
- Prebelievers who express an interest in church affiliation
- Prebelievers who have a history of church affiliation
- New believers who are just starting their faith journey
- Believers who are struggling with personal or family faith issues
- New church attendees who are in need of friendship
- People who have been on a prayer list
- Small-group attendees who express spiritual needs

Friendships are intentional relationships. And they are strengthened one step at a time. Your first meeting with a prebeliever or disciple should be more about getting acquainted than making a presentation. Get to know the person—and let the person get to know you:
- Family members (including names and ages of children)
- Family background
- Church background
- Vocation
- Hobbies
- Favorites (music, books, food, Web sites, etc.)

3. TAKE INTENTIONAL RISKS

"'Zacchaeus, come down immediately. I must stay at your house today.' So he came down at once and welcomed him gladly. All the people saw this and began to mutter, 'He has gone to be the guest of a "sinner"'" (Luke 19:5-7).

a. Jesus risked time

Notice the words "immediately" and "today." You've heard it said of someone who shows great interest in others, "They're always there when you need them." "Always" is a risky word. It means that for the sake of the relationship, a person may rearrange his or her schedule. An intentional relationship includes a willingness to spend the time necessary to let another person know you are sincerely interested in him or her.
- Give your contact information—and available times.
- Remind the person of your availability.
- Do an act of kindness when least expected (e.g., after hours or on a holiday).
- Be willing to meet at a time most convenient to the other person.

b. Jesus risked reputation

"He has gone to be the guest of a 'sinner.'" Christ's disciples should always be concerned that their attitudes and actions reflect positively on Him, avoiding the "appearance of evil." But establishing an intentional relationship with another may include going to that person's "turf." For example, you may be asked to attend a function that is totally unlike a church function, including entertainment or refreshments. Be conscious of the Holy Spirit's leadership in those situations—and never compromise

51

your standards—but if it seems the Spirit is leading you to make the contact, you can show your interest by

- Making a brief appearance at a function
- Greeting the person who invited you
- And then politely making your exit

c. Jesus risked acceptance

"Zacchaeus stood up and said to the Lord, 'Look, Lord! Here and now I give half of my possessions to the poor, and if I have cheated anybody out of anything, I will pay back four times the amount'" (Luke 19:8). Jesus accepted the tax collector's word. In working with a new disciple, the discipler must be gracious about the disciple's pledges and promises. Many are spontaneous and ill-planned but are genuine expressions. Your experience will sort them. Risk your acceptance. Build on the positive.

- Give praise for the enthusiasm.
- Give biblical examples of making covenants with God.
- Underscore God's covenant to believers.
- Guide the disciple in fleshing out promises and pledges in daily life.

d. Jesus risked forgiveness

"Jesus said to him, 'Today salvation has come to this house'" (v. 9a). In Zacchaeus's heart, there was a new beginning. Paul wrote, "Be kind to each other, tenderhearted, forgiving one another, just as God through Christ has forgiven you" (Eph. 4:32, NLT). With a prebeliever, your testimony of God's forgiveness will plant a seed of interest. With new disciples, your attitude of forgiveness and your belief that they are new persons in Christ (2 Cor. 5:17) will affirm them.

- You help them discover biblical promises of forgiveness.
- Your attitude toward them is one of restoration.
- You continually remind them that God has forgiven them.
- You compliment actions and attitudes that reflect their forgiveness.

e. Jesus risked association

"This man, too, is a son of Abraham. For the Son of Man came to seek and to save what was lost" (Luke 19:9b-10). Jesus made a bold statement—and a bold association—in front of the onlookers. Many were religious people. Some were teachers and writers of religious thought. It didn't matter who was watching, Jesus publicly identified with the tax collector Zacchaeus.

Prebelievers are often afraid to lose the emotional support of family and friends. You will need to develop your friendship with them.

(See chapter 6.)

Your acceptance and association will let them know (1) you believe in them and (2) you are their friend and fellow member of God's family. New disciples may carry a reputation with them. Your task is not to gloss over their past deeds but to help disciples get past them. Jesus exemplified that acceptance:

> Now one of the Pharisees invited Jesus to have dinner with him, so he went to the Pharisee's house and reclined at the table. When a woman who had lived a sinful life in that town learned that Jesus was eating at the Pharisee's house, she brought an alabaster jar of perfume, and as she stood behind him at his feet weeping, she began to wet his feet with her tears. Then she wiped them with her hair, kissed them and poured perfume on them. When the Pharisee who had invited him saw this, he said to himself, "If this man were a prophet, he would

know who is touching him and what kind of woman she is—that she is a sinner." Jesus answered him, "Simon, I have something to tell you." "Tell me, teacher," he said. "Two men owed money to a certain moneylender. One owed him five hundred denarii, and the other fifty. Neither of them had the money to pay him back, so he canceled the debts of both. Now which of them will love him more?" Simon replied, "I suppose the one who had the bigger debt canceled." "You have judged correctly," Jesus said. Then he turned toward the woman and said to Simon, "Do you see this woman? I came into your house. You did not give me any water for my feet, but she wet my feet with her tears and wiped them with her hair. You did not give me a kiss, but this woman, from the time I entered, has not stopped kissing my feet. You did not put oil on my head, but she has poured perfume on my feet. Therefore, I tell you, her many sins have been forgiven—for she loved much. But he who has been forgiven little loves little." Then Jesus said to her, "Your sins are forgiven" *(Luke 7:36-48)*.

4. MINISTER LIKE JESUS

Discipleship is a very personal ministry. You will be ministering to very human people who have very human characteristics. Some will fail you and others will thrill you. Some will be forever grateful and others won't even say "Thank you." Yours will not be unlike the ministry of the Master. Keep several important characteristics of that ministry in mind:

- *Jesus met people at their point of need.* "'What do you want me to do for you?' Jesus asked him. The blind man said, 'Rabbi, I want to see.' 'Go,' said Jesus, 'your faith has healed you.' Immediately he received his sight and followed Jesus along the road" (Mark 10:51-52).

- *Jesus helped people believe they could become better than they were.* "'Come, follow me,' Jesus said, 'and I will make you fishers of men'" (Matt. 4:19).

- *Jesus pointed a way out of hopeless situations.* "'Lord,' Martha said to Jesus, 'if you had been here, my brother would not have died. But I know that even now God will give you whatever you ask.' Jesus said to her, 'Your brother will rise again.' Martha answered, 'I know he will rise again in the resurrection at the last day.' Jesus said to her, 'I am the resurrection and the life. He who believes in me will live, even though he dies; and whoever lives and believes in me will never die'" (John 11:21-26).

- *Jesus never gave up on people.* "I have prayed for you, Simon, that your faith may not fail. And when you have turned back, strengthen your brothers" (Luke 22:32).

- *Jesus gave with no thought of return.* "Don't run from suffering; embrace it. Follow me and I'll show you how. Self-help is no help at all. Self-sacrifice is the way, my way, to finding yourself, your true self" (Matt. 16:25, TM).

- *Jesus always encouraged people to make the extra effort.* "If someone forces you to go one mile, go with him two miles" (Matt. 5:41).

- *Jesus relied on the Scriptures.* "It is written: 'Man does not live on bread alone, but on every word that comes from the mouth of God'" (Matt. 4:4).

- *Jesus was always on a mission.* "I must be about My Father's business" (Luke 2:49, NKJV).

- *Jesus never compromised His character.* "'All these things I will give You if You will fall down and worship me.' Then Jesus said to him, 'Away with you, Satan! For it is written, 'You shall worship the LORD your God, and Him only you shall serve'" (Matt. 4:9-10, NKJV).

- *Jesus taught with compassion.* "Then Jesus went about all the cities and villages, teaching in their synagogues, preaching the gospel of the kingdom, and healing every sickness and every

53

disease among the people. But when He saw the multitudes, He was moved with compassion for them, because they were weary and scattered, like sheep having no shepherd" (Matt. 9:35-36, NKJV).

- *Jesus lived a life of joy.* "At that time Jesus, full of joy through the Holy Spirit, said, 'I praise you, Father, Lord of heaven and earth, because you have hidden these things from the wise and learned, and revealed them to little children. Yes, Father, for this was your good pleasure'" (Luke 10:21).
- *Jesus prayed continually.* "Jesus went out to a mountainside to pray, and spent the night praying to God" (Luke 6:12).
- *Jesus observed people carefully.* "Jesus sat down opposite the place where the offerings were put and watched the crowd putting their money into the temple treasury" (Mark 12:41).
- *Jesus lived simply.* "Jesus replied, 'Foxes have holes and birds of the air have nests, but the Son of Man has no place to lay his head'" (Matt. 8:20).
- *Jesus forgave without expectations.* "Then Peter came to Jesus and asked, 'Lord, how many times shall I forgive my brother when he sins against me? Up to seven times?' Jesus answered, 'I tell you, not seven times, but seventy-seven times'" (Matt. 18:21-22).
- *Jesus obeyed the Father no matter the cost.* "Again, a second time, He went away and prayed, saying, 'O My Father, if this cup cannot pass away from Me unless I drink it, Your will be done'" (Matt. 26:42, NKJV).

The starting point of your discipleship effort is a handshake, a friendly greeting, and an encouraging word. It is a point of thankfulness to God for His trust in you and a point of trust in God for the work He will do through you.

⑪ IDENTIFY SPIRITUAL UNDERSTANDING LEVELS

Philip the disciple was on a missionary trip when he met a member of Queen Candace's royal court, who was reading the Scriptures. It turned into a discipling ministry. Acts 8:26-40 tells what happened. Notice the sequence:

(1) Philip obeyed the Spirit's leading. "Now an angel of the Lord said to Philip, 'Go south to the road—the desert road—that goes down from Jerusalem to Gaza.' So he started out, and on his way he met an Ethiopian eunuch, an important official in charge of all the treasury of Candace, queen of the Ethiopians" (vv. 26-27).

Obviously the Ethiopian was a religious man, but he didn't have the knowledge that leads to salvation. He needed a discipler. God will make the appointment; you will need to be open to His Spirit's leading.

(2) He identified a spiritual understanding level. "Then Philip ran up to the chariot and heard the man reading Isaiah the prophet. 'Do you understand what you are reading?' Philip asked. 'How can I,' he said, 'unless someone explains it to me?'" (vv. 30-31). The disciple's helpful attitude reflected the concern of his heart. But to provide the spiritual help needed, he had to discover the official's level of spiritual understanding.

His question, "Do you understand what you are reading?" led to important insights into the man's religious experience. Similar questions (and answers) will give you an insight not only into a person's familiarity with the Bible but also into his or her spiritual interests.

(3) He taught him from his level of understanding. "'Tell me, please, who is the prophet talking about, himself or someone else?' Then Philip began with that very passage of Scripture and told him the good news about Jesus" (vv. 34-35). He discovered an entry level and began to teach accordingly.

(4) He encouraged him to the next level. "As they traveled along the road, they came to some water and the eunuch said, 'Look, here is water. Why shouldn't I be baptized?' And he gave orders to stop the chariot. Then both Philip and the eunuch went down into the water and Philip baptized him" (vv. 36-38). For him, baptism might have been simply another ritual in his ritual-filled religion. But surely the apostle would have spent time explaining that baptism was more than a ceremony; it was a symbol of repentance and faith—and turning from his old ways to a new life of faith.

Part of the discipler's task is to encourage the disciple to the next level of commitment. To help the person understand the importance of religious practices in light of being born again or of being sanctified.

(5) He released him. "When they came up out of the water, the Spirit of the Lord suddenly took Philip away, and the eunuch did not see him again, but went on his way rejoicing. Philip, however, appeared at Azotus and traveled about, preaching the gospel in all the towns until he reached Caesarea" (vv. 39-40). Phillip had an initial assignment, carried out the assignment, and then let the new disciple discover some truth on his own. Discipleship has both short-range and long-range dimensions.

- The level of understanding is established.
- An initial learning path is determined.
- At the appropriate time, new disciples are trusted to make some discoveries on their own—yet remaining on the prayer list and contact list of the discipler.

LEVELS OF UNDERSTANDING

Philip's discipleship encounter teaches about the importance of discerning the spiritual needs of others. As a discipler you will need to know where to begin—and what teaching path to take as a result. Consider at least three levels of spiritual understanding and a proposed teaching path for people in each of those levels.

Level one: the prebeliever

With over 4 billion people in the world who are classified as non-Christian, there is a great need to lead people to a decision to follow Jesus Christ. Christ himself taught us about reaching out to people in the scriptural account of the meeting with the Samaritan woman at the well: John 4:4-30.

Notice how Jesus presented important truth to her:

(a) He established an intentional friendship. "When a Samaritan woman came to draw water, Jesus said to her, 'Will you give me a drink?' (His disciples had gone into the town to buy food.) The Samaritan woman said to him, 'You are a Jew and I am a Samaritan woman. How can you ask me for a drink?' (For Jews do not associate with Samaritans)" (vv. 7-9).

Jesus took the most important risk: He met the Samaritan at her point of need, no matter the opinion of others. One-on-one evangelism is never outdated. Jesus established the method, and it will always be an important part of the discipleship process.

Meeting people at their point of need begins with establishing an "intentional friendship" that has the goal of presenting the gospel. Some conversation starters may include

- Religious affiliation
- Social issues and their relationship to faith
- Opinions about God
- World situations

Responses will give insights into the person's level of spiritual understanding. For example, a person's opinion about God will indicate whether he or she has knowledge of the Bible, whether he or she has a "worldview" (atheistic, agnostic, pluralistic, etc.) opinion, or whether he or she has personal or spiritual issues about his or her relationship with God.

(b) He developed an interest. "Jesus answered her, 'If you knew the gift of God and who it is that asks you for a drink, you would have asked him and he would have given you living water.' 'Sir,' the woman said, 'you have nothing to draw with and the well is deep. Where can you get this living water?'" (vv. 10-11).

Two met at that well. One was the sinless Son of God, the Creator of the universe, and the other was an adulteress. They were eternities apart, but they met at the same well. It was a meeting that was ordained in heaven. Making a friendship link means sharing a point of common interest. In this situation the common interest was a drink of water. It was an easy link to the most pressing needs—forgiveness and salvation. Her interest in His message was sparked by the words, "If you only knew." Immediately she understood that something was missing in her life.

In your situation the common interest might be such things as sports or handicrafts or business or travel. The subject was water, but it was merely a link to the more important subject—the condition of the woman's soul.

(c) He made a thought-provoking statement. "He told her, 'Go, call your husband and come back.' 'I have no husband,' she replied. Jesus said to her, 'You are right when you say you have no husband. The fact is, you have had five husbands, and the man you now have is not your husband. What you have just said is quite true'" (vv. 16-18).

Jesus knew her condition before He ever inquired about her relationships. Jesus brought the woman to a point of admitting her need. She had to come face-to-face with the standard of God's Word.

Prebelievers must be led to look at their condition in relation to the holiness of God and the truth of God's Word. The need of a Savior can't be seen until there is an understanding of the hopelessness of sin (Rom. 6:23).

(d) He gave her a glimpse of hope. "A time is coming and has now come when the true worshipers will worship the Father in spirit and truth, for they are the kind of worshipers the Father seeks. God is spirit, and his worshipers must worship in spirit and in truth" (vv. 23-24).

Jesus showed her a better way. The gospel is a message of hope. God's love made a way of escape. People don't have to be lost in sin. They can be "found" in salvation.

(e) He taught her about the truth of God's Word. "Then Jesus declared, 'I who speak to you am he'" (v. 26).

Jesus revealed the eternal truth that He is the Messiah. One-on-one discipleship is leading a person to an encounter with the claims of the Word of God.

The outcome was life-changing for the woman. She came to the well thirsting but left forgiven. A directed conversation was a teaching path that led to her conversion.

Level two: new believer

The next level of spiritual understanding is seen in the life of one who has recently made a decision to follow Christ. That person may, or may not, understand who Christ is and what His teachings include.

The local church may have a program of assigning a spiritual mentor-discipler to the new believer. That discipler should have some basic qualities:

- A disciple of good reputation in the church
- A member of the local church
- A proven "track record" of working with people
- A proven knowledge of the Scriptures and doctrinal beliefs
- A willingness to go the extra mile in fulfilling an assignment

The disciple Ananias's spiritual mentoring of Saul (later named Paul) is a gold standard: Acts 9:10-20. Because of Ananias's patient teaching/mentoring/discipling of the former persecutor of Christians, the Church has, through Paul's writings, some of the most practical and powerful teachings on the Christian life. Ananias drops off the charts after discipling the new believer, Saul, but who could doubt that he did the job right?

(a) He took the risk. "The Lord told him, 'Go to the house of Judas on Straight Street and ask for a man from Tarsus named Saul, for he is praying. In a vision he has seen a man named Ananias come and place his hands on him to restore his sight.' 'Lord,' Ananias answered, 'I have heard many reports about this man and all the harm he has done to your saints in Jerusalem'" (vv. 11-13).

Ananias had heard about Saul's former lifestyle. He knew that he had been a persecutor of Christians. He knew that Saul was a highly educated man, who probably knew more about the Scriptures. But he was compelled by the Holy Spirit to take on the assignment—no matter the personal cost.

Discipleship is often costly.

- It takes time.
- It takes preparation.
- It takes patience.
- It sometimes takes a financial commitment.

But the result is worth the investment.

(b) He approached him. "Then Ananias went to the house and entered it. Placing his hands on Saul, he said, 'Brother Saul . . .'" (v. 17*ab*).

Ananias greeted Saul with a heartwarming greeting, "Brother Saul." It was an immediate bridge of friendship. By greeting him as his brother, Ananias was letting Saul know they were on common ground. Their qualifications, their lifestyles, their spiritual understanding level were of little importance now. They were brothers in Christ.

Saul was probably just as hesitant as Ananias. His whole world had been turned upside down. We don't know the reason or the extent of Saul's blindness, but we can only imagine that it was very frustrating. He needed a friend. He needed Ananias.

New believers face similar changes. In one sense, their new life in Christ is a step into the unknown.

- There is a break with the past.
- They often risk broken relationships with family or former friends.
- Their associates may not understand their decision to follow Christ.
- They become a part of a whole new "family."
- They are introduced to a new belief system.
- They are faced with understanding the Scriptures.
- They often have to familiarize themselves with new worship forms.
- They struggle with temptations to revert to their former ways.

Your task as a discipler is to approach the new disciple with a spirit of openness and friendship, letting the person know that you are concerned about his or her new transition.

(c) He taught him. "'Jesus, who appeared to you on the road as you were coming here—has sent me so that you may see again and be filled with the Holy Spirit.' Immediately, something like scales fell from Saul's eyes, and he could see again. He got up and was baptized" (vv. 17*c*-18).

Ananias began to explain "the Way" to Saul.

- He familiarized him with the basics of the Christian faith.
- He advised him on Christian ethics and a Christian lifestyle.
- He encouraged him to use his education, knowledge, and skills in ministry.

(d) He released him. "After taking some food, he regained his strength. Saul spent several days with the disciples in Damascus. At once he began to preach in the synagogues that Jesus is the Son of God" (vv. 19-20).

Ananias wasn't threatened by Paul's abilities; he recognized they were God-given and served God's master plan for the Church. He mentored the new believer and then released him to work. Once a discipleship process has been completed—and sometimes even *during*—a new believer can be strengthened by a guided involvement in ministry.

- Make sure the ministry is fully *explained.*
- Make sure the "minister" is fully *trained.*
- Make sure the ministry isn't *strained* (not beyond the person's skill level).

Level three: Uncommitted or unassigned believer

You may be asked to encourage more established believers to make a next-level commitment. That assignment may be carried out in several settings:

- Small groups
- Church administration

- Volunteer ministries
- Mission trips

You will be asked to encourage fellow believers to use their spiritual gifts in ministry to others. You may also be asked to encourage a fellow believer to make a stronger commitment to the local church through church membership.

Aquila and Priscilla were members of the Early Church who made *next-level* commitments (Acts 18:1-26). Paul (formerly Saul) saw they had great potential to be ministers and disciplers. Like Paul, they were tradespeople who used a tent-making business not only to support themselves but also as a means of supporting their church fellowship. He could identify with them and personally encouraged them toward ministry.

- *He befriended them.* "Paul went to see them, and because he was a tentmaker as they were, he stayed and worked with them" (vv. 2-3).

There was not only a common vocational link but also a spiritual link. Aquila and Priscilla were not uncommitted in their faith; they were just unassigned. Paul's influence began with a common-ground friendship.

- *He mentored them.* "Every Sabbath he reasoned in the synagogue, trying to persuade Jews and Greeks" (v. 4).

They were encouraged by their on-the-job experience in ministry with Paul. Some of the best soul winners, for example, have "caught" their enthusiasm for leading others to Christ by witnessing the ministry of a soul winner. Paul used the skills and commitment of Aquila and Priscilla by taking them with him and using them in ministry to others.

- *He launched them.* "They arrived at Ephesus, where Paul left Priscilla and Aquila. He himself went into the synagogue and reasoned with the Jews" (v. 19).

Following his discipling, mentoring, and interning process, Paul gave the couple a place of service. They became leaders in their own right. The principles and passions of the apostle Paul were integrated in their own ministry. Your task is not only to teach the new disciples the "principles of flight" but also to encourage them to "fly." Just as a mother bird encourages the baby chick to abandon the nest, you have the opportunity to launch a ministry.

⑫ SUPPLY A SUPPORT SYSTEM

Encouraging the disciple to a next-level commitment takes a focused and purposeful effort. The time and effort will vary from one person to another, but the basic qualities of commitment, concern, communication, and concentrated training must be present in each discipleship assignment. Those qualities should be present in a support system for your disciple, no matter his or her level of spiritual understanding. Let's take a look at a sample system for the new believer and the believer who has made a recent or renewed commitment.

1. NEW BELIEVER

The new birth is a cornerstone of biblical truth. Every discipleship effort is based on the biblical fact that we are born with a tendency to sin (Rom. 5:12), that the penalty of sin is spiritual death (6:23), and that the death and resurrection of Jesus Christ made it possible for us to be born again spiritually, through faith in Him (Eph. 2:5). "'How can a man be born when he is old?' Nicodemus asked. 'Surely he cannot enter a second time into his mother's womb to be born!' Jesus answered, 'I tell you the truth, no one can enter the kingdom of God unless he is born of water and the Spirit. Flesh gives birth to flesh, but the Spirit gives birth to spirit. You should not be surprised at my saying, "You must be born again"'" (John 3:4-7).

The apostle Paul called the disciple Timothy his "son" in the faith. In that sense, discipling a new believer might be compared to a parent's care for a newborn child.

And if we think of new believers in that context—no matter their age or knowledge—there are several skills that are important not only for survival but also for development. The Mayo Clinic identified four areas of development in the infant: motor skills, hearing, vision, and communication.[11]

While our discipleship efforts will not be focused on children, youth, or adults, some of the same principles of development may be applied. Those principles are seen in the apostle Paul's prayers for his disciples:

a. Motor skills: building movement and coordination

> For this reason, since the day we heard about you, we have not stopped praying for you and asking God to fill you with the knowledge of his will through all spiritual wisdom and understanding. And we pray this in order that you may live a life worthy of the Lord and may please him in every way: bearing fruit in every good work, growing in the knowledge of God, being strengthened with all power according to his glorious might so that you may have great endurance and patience, and joyfully giving thanks to the Father, who has qualified you to share in the inheritance of the saints in the kingdom of light *(Col. 1:9-12)*.

Paul was concerned about the forward movement of those in his care. His prayer reflects his concern that the disciples of Christ develop in their spiritual motor skills.

(1) **He prayed for their growth in knowledge.** "Asking God to fill you with the knowledge of his will through all spiritual wisdom and understanding" (v. 9). Physiologically, forward movement results from brain impulses. Spiritually, forward movement results from inner spirit impulses. Paul not only prayed that the Holy Spirit would impress biblical truth on their minds but also gave them access to that truth. Similarly as a discipler you are a guide, leading your disciple along the paths of biblical truth. Supply your disciple with a support system of Bible study.

A regular (perhaps weekly) Bible study with your disciple is one of the best ways to share the knowledge of God's Word with him or her. The Bible study times should be *(a)* agreed upon in advance regarding time and length, *(b)* regularly conducted, *(c)* brief but thorough in scope, *(d)* include a review and assignments, and *(e)* have an end date in mind.

- Use the basic Bible study provided by your denomination.
- Choose a book of the Bible that introduces Christ and His message (Gospel of John?).
- Study a Bible character to whom your disciple might relate (Ruth?).
- Focus on a subject (Forgiveness?).

Whether you meet in the home, at a restaurant, or on the church property, your faithfulness in teaching the Bible will be reflected in the growth of your disciple. Some guidelines:

- *Don't be afraid of questions.* "I'll get back to you on that" should be a natural response for questions that may be out of your expertise. Don't be intimidated by a question for which you don't have an answer. Remember, your disciple probably knows far less about the Bible than you may think!

- *Don't be sidetracked by personal issues.* Often a Bible study participant will bring up issues that might relate to bad experiences in the church or in other Christian organizations. "Let's put that question on hold for now. I think some of those questions will be answered later in our study" should suffice.

- *Don't assume that your student knows how to get around in the Bible.* The basics of the Bible's table of contents, study helps, and concordance should be included up front. Knowing there is a page number for a book of the Bible, for example, could be just the thing to put a new believer at ease.

- *Don't tackle the "big ones."* For example, your student may suggest a study of the Book of Revelation as a first choice. Tackling a more difficult book of the Bible to interpret, such as Revelation or Daniel, would be better reserved for a later study.

- *Don't give up.* The Holy Spirit will guide your student into truth. At times it may seem that your student is not making progress. God's Word will always have an effect: "So is my word that goes out from my mouth: It will not return to me empty, but will accomplish what I desire and achieve the purpose for which I sent it" (Isa. 55:11).

(2) **He prayed for their growth in character.** "And we pray this in order that you may live a life worthy of the Lord and may please him in every way: bearing fruit in every good work" (Col. 1:10). Coordination skills are important to development. Paul was concerned that Christians be steady in their walk. He knew how vulnerable disciples were to the influences of the world and knew that only a change of heart would result in a change of lifestyle. Paul prayed that his disciples would learn to be leaders and not followers. He even had the courage to say "Follow me as I follow Christ." A life well lived would be a living example of the grace of God. As a discipler, you have an opportunity to encourage your disciple to live a life that honors Christ—one that reflects good spiritual coordination.

- *Guard your own heart.* Pray for God's wisdom and strength in facing the influence of the world. Live an exemplary life before your disciple—including refraining from being judgmental or critical of others.

- *Trust the Spirit's conviction.* A host of dos and don'ts may "bruise the fruit." Trust the Holy Spirit to use the truth of the Word to give direction for lifestyle choices. Disciples may have addictions or habits that are not only psychological but also physiological. A pledge to pray with them about a certain practice is better than chastising them.

- *Point out the good.* There are people in your fellowship who are making a difference for

Christ. Use them as teaching examples. But always remind your disciple to focus on Jesus rather than on people, because people often make mistakes but Jesus doesn't.

(3) He prayed for their strong finish. "Being strengthened with all power according to his glorious might so that you may have great endurance and patience, and joyfully giving thanks to the Father, who has qualified you to share in the inheritance of the saints in the kingdom of light" (vv. 11-12). Let disciples know that God's power is greater than what may happen to them or come against them. Be positive. Trust God for their great finish. Point out the hope, even over the headlines. Remind them of the finish—heaven.

b. Hearing: responding to voices and other sounds

> Now we pray to God that you will not do anything wrong. Not that people will see that we have stood the test but that you will do what is right even though we may seem to have failed. For we cannot do anything against the truth, but only for the truth. We are glad whenever we are weak but you are strong; and our prayer is for your perfection *(2 Cor. 13:7-9)*.

Just as responding to voices of parental authority is a sign of physical development, so obedient responses to God is a sign of spiritual development. Paul understood how dependent he was on the power of the Holy Spirit for victorious living. He wanted his disciples to trust in God's power, not human effort. Disciples will be subject to the accusing "whispers" of the enemy, Satan (Rev. 12:10). It will be your task to help them learn how to discern between the leadership of the Spirit and the temptations of the enemy. Even as you pray for their spiritual victory, you will need to provide them with a support system of spiritual discernment.

- Teach them that God never speaks contrary to His Word.
- Teach them that God never leads contrary to their conscience.
- Teach them that God uses the counsel of other Christians to advise them.
- Teach them that God can even use adversity to strengthen them.

(1) Your availability to them when they are facing tempting times will be a great source of encouragement and strength. Reinforce their good decisions. Review their unwise decisions, discovering with them in a spirit of affirmation how much difference being obedient to the Word of God would have made.

- Yours is a shoulder to lean upon.
- Yours is a hand that reaches out.
- Yours are feet that run to them in their time of need.
- Your testimony of God's blessing for obedience is one that will help them be good "listeners."

And your "system" of providing contact information for times of prayer in emergency situations will let them know that you really care about them.

(2) Also, let them know how human you are. Don't hide the fact that you haven't always obeyed, that you have misread spiritual signals, and that you are still learning to discern. Paul was very open about his weakness in the face of the enemy's attack. But his openness was also a sign of strength. He told his disciples that his weakness was a stepping-stone for them. Others would learn by his spiritual journey.

(3) Encourage disciples to a life of holiness.

- Provide literature and a study that will teach them about entire sanctification.
- Share your testimony of how you discovered the power of Spirit-filled living (Acts 1:8) and what a difference it has made in your life.
- Teach them that God has already provided a way to be free from the rebellious nature they were born with, through the sanctifying work of the Cross (Heb. 9:14).

c. Vision: learning to focus

> I pray also that the eyes of your heart may be enlightened in order that you may know the hope to which he has called you, the riches of his glorious inheritance in the saints, and his incomparably great power for us who believe. That power is like the working of his mighty strength, which he exerted in Christ when he raised him from the dead and seated him at his right hand in the heavenly realms, far above all rule and authority, power and dominion, and every title that can be given, not only in the present age but also in the one to come *(Eph. 1:18-21)*.

Paul was a purpose-driven man (Phil. 3:13-14). His whole life was one of pursuing the goal. And to do that, he had to forget what was behind. He encouraged those whom he led to focus their attention on the eternal, not the earthly; on the future rather than the past.

(1) He prayed that they would be people of a clean heart. "I pray also that the eyes of your heart may be enlightened" (v. 18*a*). He prayed that their hearts would be free from the clutter of the world so that the light of the world, Jesus Christ, could shine in. A heart that is focused wholly on Christ is free to choose life. Death no longer has dominion over it. Personal claims have been surrendered. Repentance has resulted in forgiveness. Despair has given way to hope.

Help disciples learn how to focus on Christ:

* Inform them about alternative Christian entertainment.
* Take them to a Christian bookstore to review available resources.
* Give them information about Christian support groups.
* Advise them of Christian Internet sites and resources.
* Take them to Christian concert or drama events.

They will need to see the "other side of the fence"—the Christian side. They will need to know that being a Christian is not a drab and boring lifestyle; rather there are a variety of quality options.

(2) He prayed that they would know about true riches. "That you may know the hope to which he has called you, the riches of his glorious inheritance in the saints" (v. 18*bc*). Your disciple lives in a world that trusts in riches. You will need to explain that true material goods are simply God's blessings on loan. He is the true owner. Everything we are and everything we have belongs to Him. Paul wanted those whom he taught to know that the "best is yet to come." He wanted them to fix their eyes on the finish line—not the race.

You can make a distinct difference in your disciple's worldview through what you teach:

* Teach about God's ownership.
* Teach about giving back to God.
* Teach about the principle of the tithe.
* Teach about the hope of eternal life.
* Teach about making earthly investments of time, talent, treasure.

(3) He prayed that they would understand Christ's rule. "The working of his mighty strength, which he exerted in Christ when he raised him from the dead and seated him at his right hand in the heavenly realms, far above all rule and authority." (vv. 19*b*-21*a*). Paul wanted the church to understand that it was on the winning side! He wanted believers to know that the One who created the world is still Ruler over it. He wanted the people of God to know that Christ will be the final Victor.

Disciples live in an overwhelming setting. The forces of hell are being unleashed against the Church. They must know that God will have the last say in the affairs of the world. They must know that the outcome has already been settled (John 19:30).

* Offer recommended literature and study on Bible prophecy.

- Take them to a recommended conference or seminar that focuses on Bible prophecy.
- Involve them in reading some prophetic books in the Bible.
- Give them a testimony of your own hope in the "final outcome."
- Remind them to pray for persecuted brothers and sisters in Christ.

d. Communication: expressing affection

And this is my prayer: that your love may abound more and more in knowledge and depth of insight, so that you may be able to discern what is best and may be pure and blameless until the day of Christ, filled with the fruit of righteousness that comes through Jesus Christ—to the glory and praise of God *(Phil. 1:9-11)*.

As a newborn develops a response to the affection and affirmation of its family, new believers develop responses of affection and affirmation to their new spiritual family. Paul was concerned that the disciples understood the depths of commitment and interdependence that come with being a part of God's family. He wanted them to have pure intentions in all matters of the heart.

For the most part disciples have entered a whole new atmosphere of family relationships. Christianity includes the emotions as well as the will. Emotional feelings will be an integral part of worship and fellowship. Your task is to guide disciples in making wise decisions about their emotional attachments in their relationships.

- Encourage them to express their affection and affirmation in positive ways. Give them advice about their relationships with Christians of the opposite sex.
- Help them to set ethical boundaries in their ministries to those who are underage.
- Caution them about the potential dangers of personal counseling sessions. And help them to understand that their best ministry in most situations would be to refer a troubled fellow believer to a professional counselor or pastoral staff member.
- Promote their involvement in building up the family of God through notes, e-mail, or text messages of encouragement, while advising them about crossing emotional boundary lines.
- Help them understand that the devil would use innocent remarks or gestures to bring ruin to them personally or to their family.

Your task is to set up a support system that will mainstream them into the church fellowship.

- Invite them to church fellowship events.
- Acquaint them with Christian friends who might have similar interests.
- Encourage them to participate in compassionate ministries.
- Make them aware of national or international mission trips.
- Set an example in showing your support for them by regular contact.

2. NEWLY COMMITTED BELIEVER

A discipler is also a coach. He or she provides training and guidance for committed believers who have taken next-level steps of growth or ministry. Again, the ministry of Ananias to Saul (later known as Paul) serves as a reminder of coaching principles. That ministry, as you remember, included intentional friendship, training, and advice. Those newly committed believers, whose active ministry has been dormant, may or may not have prior knowledge or skills for their assigned tasks. As a discipler-coach you will need to discover the believer's

- Level of spiritual understanding
- Personal experience
- Character traits

- Readiness for assignment

As a member of your church or organization's ministry team, you may be asked to coach a newly committed believer for a new assignment. You will design a support system for the assignment. Your first responsibility is to pray for the believer. When the tasks of caring for the Early Church membership took time from their spiritual preparation, the apostles sought ministry helpers:

> "Brothers, choose seven men from among you who are known to be full of the Spirit and wisdom. We will turn this responsibility over to them and will give our attention to prayer and the ministry of the word." This proposal pleased the whole group. They chose Stephen, a man full of faith and of the Holy Spirit; also Philip, Procorus, Nicanor, Timon, Parmenas, and Nicolas from Antioch, a convert to Judaism. They presented these men to the apostles, who prayed and laid their hands on them *(Acts 6:3-6)*.

The disciples knew that the blessing of God must be a priority. The greater part of your disciple-coaching ministry will be to pray for the one under your supervision. Your prayer partnership with your disciple will be an investment he or she will treasure. And besides, your prayers are weapons against the forces of hell that will try to ruin your disciple's assignment—and your disciple.

But you should also be knowledgeable of the disciple's qualifications for the assigned task.

a. Try to determine the disciple's level of spiritual understanding

Is the disciple spiritually prepared for the assignment? Of course only God knows the heart; but evidence of the fruits of the Spirit (Gal. 5) will indicate whether the candidate is spiritually mature enough to accomplish the ministry.

Another indicator is the person's obvious knowledge of the Bible and biblical doctrine. Paul advised, "Never be in a hurry about appointing a church leader" (1 Tim. 5:22, NLT). Those seeking appointment that lack spiritual maturity can not only bring harm to others but also jeopardize their own spiritual welfare. They may be encouraged to

- Continue in a one-on-one or group Bible study.
- Take a leadership class.
- Serve as a coworker with a more mature disciple.

Your mission as a discipler-coach is to offer prayerful guidance, along with encouragement. You can reinforce your disciple's interest while offering further training.

b. Evaluate the disciple's personal experience

65

Is the disciple personally qualified for the assignment? What spiritual gifts does the person have that relate to the assignment? Someone may have an interest in a certain ministry but does not have accompanying skills. The outcome will be frustrating to the persons to whom the disciple is ministering, and it will be frustrating to the disciple personally. You can assist in matching the disciple with a ministry:

- Lead the disciple in a spiritual gifts Bible study.
- Give the disciple an opportunity to take a spiritual gifts survey.
- Encourage the disciple to look for spiritual gifts in the lives of other disciples.
- Carefully explain the job description for the ministry, along with the necessary qualifications.

The bottom line is that the Holy Spirit is the giver of spiritual gifts—himself being the greatest gift! He will lead both you and the ministry candidate in the right ministry direction. Again, your intercessory prayer for the disciple will be used of God in leading him or her into active Christian service.

c. Observe personal characteristics

Does the personality of the disciple match the assignment? For example, an assignment to serve in the church nursery or toddler department would not be in anyone's best interest if that disciple is not comfortable being around children or if he or she struggles with patience issues. Is the ministry candidate locked in to a generational mind-set? Someone who is "living in the '50s," for instance, might not be the best match for 21st-century youth ministry.

The Holy Spirit will help you discern the characteristics of your disciple that are not a good fit for the task at hand. A prayerful, careful, and affirming guidance will help your disciple toward a "cutting edge" service for Christ.

d. Evaluate the disciple's readiness

Is the disciple ready for a ministry assignment? What are the personal or family issues that would disqualify that person from immediate service?

- Schedule conflicts
- Child care conflicts
- Financial or legal issues
- Gender issues
- Relational issues
- Spiritual issues

Encourage your disciple to settle any issues first before taking on an assignment that might create additional hardships.

You are the coach. You know which player should be on the field and which player should wait on the bench for a while. You know which player is fitted to which play. Your role as a discipler-coach is to build the disciple up with training and then release that person for service with encouragement and affirmation.

The results will be heartwarming. You will multiply your own ministry many times over through the dedicated service of one in whom you have invested your life.

⑬ CONTACT REGARDING SPIRITUAL PROGRESS/NEEDS

In emergency care there is a window of time known as the golden hour, where patients under treatment have the greatest likelihood of survival. In photography, the golden hour is the first and last hour of sunlight, when a photographic effect is best achieved. Disciplers also have a window of opportunity to give focused care to those whom they are discipling. Galatians 6:9 says, "Let us not become weary in doing good, for at the proper time we will reap a harvest if we do not give up." Two familiar concepts immediately come to mind: first, *persistence pays,* "We will reap a harvest if we do not give up"; second, *timing is everything,* "at the proper time."

1. GOLDEN HOUR CONTACTS

Continuing the "care of newborns" analogy, good parenting means regularly checking the progress or needs of the child. It's the same for discipling people of all ages. There is a window of opportunity, a "golden hour," when focused care is crucial to the spiritual survival of the disciple or when the desired spiritual effect is best achieved.

We can take the golden hour a step farther. Even though each disciple is unique, there is a common concept that will insure at least a minimum amount of care time: *the golden hour—an accumulated 60 minutes of focused contact time each week.* Several means of communication may be included in the "golden hour" contact time:

- Telephone call
- E-mail, text message (and instant message)
- Note or card
- Personal appointment
- Relational event

2. CONTACT PROTOCOL

Making contacts with your disciple may cause more problems than solutions unless some parameters are observed:

a. Build a quality relationship

A positive, honest, and sincere interest in the disciple will help build a spiritual bond. If you sense that your disciple is hesitant (e.g., putting off the contact or not providing contact information) about the contact, it would be wise to pull back and to wait for the relationship to develop further.

b. Anything that is said to be "off the record" should be exactly that

Betraying confidence is the quickest way to end your relationship and to bring emotional or spiritual harm to the disciple. If someone asks you to keep something in confidence, don't even tell your spouse or best friend. *Of course in some situations, there are overriding, legal obligations.* For instance, if someone admits to illegal behavior, especially as it may relate to a minor, the confidence rule is out the window. You may have a legal obligation to advise the authorities.

c. Keep the relationship on the level

If there is any sense of an emotional attachment that could lead to breaking a moral or spiritual law, the assignment should be immediately reconsidered. Dealing with people on a personal level may lead to misunderstood words or actions. The Bible says to "abstain from all appearance of evil" (1 Thess. 5:22, KJV). Even the place and time of your meetings with a disciple should be carefully considered.

d. Make sure the contacts have time parameters

If someone whom you are discipling seems to indicate the need for a lengthier contact time, then you will need to be flexible—within reason. On the other hand, if the disciple seems to be hurried, you will not want to invade his or her "space."

e. Use the type of contact that fits the disciple

For example, if your disciple is younger, you may want to use electronic mail, text messaging, or instant messaging for quick contacts—and the telephone for longer. Depending on the tech skill level of the disciple, you will soon discover his or her contact preference.

f. Make sure the contact has an end goal of spiritual growth

Using a contact for making a political or social statement should be avoided. Also, you should never reflect negatively on a church or another Christian—including church leadership.

3. CONTACT METHODS

Various communication media may be used to let others know you are interested in them and are there for them in time of need. Remember, the objective is to observe the *golden hour, a minimum of 60 minutes per week in contact time with your disciple.*

a. Telephone call

A friendly voice is still one of the most effective ways to share Christ's love. Several things should be kept in mind:

(1) **Make sure a telephone call is welcomed.** In some situations, a phone call would be an intrusion (e.g., work hours or family time). Ask for the disciple's contact information—including his or her address, cell phone or home phone numbers, and e-mail address. If there is a hesitancy to give out phone numbers, for instance, ask for the most convenient way for you to stay in touch.

(2) **Make brevity your goal.** Ten to 15 minutes can be adequate. Some situations will take longer. But in your mind, set a goal of making a brief but focused call. Remember, your purpose in calling is, *(a)* to express your concern, *(b)* to check on progress or needs, and *(c)* to strengthen an intentional relationship.

(3) **Prayerfully think about what you will say.** No, you won't need a script (unless you've made some notes about a Bible study or a meeting time). But simply giving prayerful thought to what you might say—including a Bible verse that you may want to share—will make the call more meaningful.

(4) **Make it a friendly call.** ("Hi, Tony, I wanted to give you a call and let you know that I've been praying for you today. . . .")

(5) **Make it a purposeful call.** ("How is everything, Tony? Do you have any questions about last week's Bible study? Is there something you would like me to join with you in prayer about?")

- Listen for the tone of voice (positive, negative, upset, or angry).
- Respond according to the tone of the conversation.
- List prayer requests, and later remind your disciple that you prayed about the requests.

- Pick out an encouraging Bible verse (in advance) and quote it.
- Ask if a book, chapter, or verse from the Bible has especially impacted the disciple this week.
- Remind your disciple that you are continually praying for him or her.

Consistent contact is the immediate objective.

b. E-mail or text messaging

Other effective methods of communicating with your disciple may include e-mailing or text messaging. Age and skill levels may be a deciding factor, but their widespread use makes them valuable.

(1) E-mail

- Make sure your disciple's e-mail address is a personal rather than business address.
- Don't "copy" your messages to others.
- Prayerfully think about the content.
- Make the message brief.
- Be consistent.
- Be positive.
- Limit the e-mails to one or two each week.
- Avoid including or attaching "pass-along" content (jokes, cartoons, petitions, poems, rumors, political messages, racial content, etc.).
- Include a Bible verse.
- Check for grammar and spelling.
- Remind your disciple of your prayers.
- Remind your disciple of your availability.

(2) Text message

- Avoid "cutesy" content.
- Get right to the point.
- Remind your disciple of your prayers.
- Include a Scripture reference rather than an entire verse (e.g., John 3:16).
- Be consistent.
- Limit the number of messages.

Instant messages (IM) or video conferencing may also be used to make a contact. God has provided ways to communicate His Word that transcend the barriers of four walls or even geographical boundaries. Prayerfully use the media, keeping in mind that the airwaves are open to monitoring and abuse.

c. Note or card

No matter how technology progresses, a hard-copy note or postcard still makes a difference! God first used "hard copy" to express His care.

- He carved His law in tablets of stone: the Ten Commandments.
- His promise of salvation through the Messiah Jesus Christ was penned by prophets onto scrolls of parchment.
- The history of the Church was handed down through generations in "hard copy."
- Handwritten copies of the Bible have been passed around prison cells and within the walls of underground churches.

The use of notes or cards isn't a matter of "instead of"; it is rather a matter of "along with." Heaven didn't need the Internet to share the greatest news ever. A chorus of angels gave the "news alert" over the airwaves of a Judean night that Christ the Savior was born in Bethlehem! God can use any—and every—media to let everyone on the planet know He loves them so much He gave His only Son to give them the hope of salvation.

Both e-cards and printed cards can be used with great effectiveness. Remember to use cards that are appropriate to your assignment (e.g., not cutesy or gaudy).

(1) Use notes or cards for encouraging or recognizing a milestone

For example, a birthday or anniversary card may include a personal note of congratulations plus a reminder of a spiritual birthday or anniversary. Here are some guidelines for hard-copy notes:

- Make sure the note/card is of good quality.
- Print rather than use cursive to make the message more legible.
- Check for the right address (and spelling).
- Check to see if sufficient postage is affixed.
- Avoid cluttering the envelope or front of card with stick-ons.
- Include your name and address.

A note or card may also be used as congratulations for a job promotion or as a way of staying in contact while you are on vacation.

(2) A note or card may be used for teaching and strengthening

Dear Nancy,

Thank you for being a part of our Bible study. I thank God for your faithfulness in attending the studies and for the contribution you make to the discussion. Wasn't that a great study on God's forgiveness? "If we confess our sins, he is faithful and just and will forgive . . ." (1 John 1:9). That's a promise! Praise the Lord for what He has done in your life! You're in my prayers.

Shelley

(3) A note or card may be used in a time of crisis

Gary,

I was so sorry to hear about the job layoff. These must be frustrating days for you and your family. But you can be sure that God is still working in your life. He often uses these times to draw us closer to Him. You are a part of His great big family. And as a member of that family with you, I want you to know that I'm praying for you. If there is anything I can do, please let me know.

Brian

(4) A note or card may be used to reinforce service

Debbie,

I was so pleased to see you help with the Christmas program. Finding a place to serve in the church is so important to growing in Christ. Thank you for letting God use you in this way. I am praying for you (Heb. 6:10).

Marie

(5) A note or card may be used to give assurance

Chad,

Just a note to tell you how grateful I am for the way the Lord is helping you grow in your faith. These are uncertain times for all of us. But we can be certain about one thing: He hasn't forgotten us (1 Cor. 10:13).

Tom

(6) A note or card may be used to congratulate a spiritual milestone

Amanda,

Witnessing your baptism was thrilling for me! I am so proud of your walk with the Lord.

You are living proof of His power to make a new creation (2 Cor. 5:17). You will be continually in my prayers.

Becky

(7) A note or card may be used to recognize an award

Josh,

All American! That's too cool! I'm really proud of you. I can't even imagine how much effort you must have put into this football season. But you can be sure that a lot of people, including me, were praying for you. Your witness to the team and to the community is a real blessing to me.

Sam

d. Personal appointment

Spending time with your disciple will be an integral part of your *golden hour* contact time. It was God's way: "But when the time had fully come, God sent his Son, born of a woman, born under law, to redeem those under law, that we might receive the full rights of sons. Because you are sons, God sent the Spirit of his Son into our hearts, the Spirit who calls out, 'Abba, Father'" (Gal. 4:4-6).

Some of Jesus' most memorable discipling was one-on-one:

- Nicodemus
- Zacchaeus
- Peter
- Mary and Martha

There are so many distractions in life. To zero-in on personal needs, it is sometimes best to get away from it all. And those same distractions make it challenging to set up personal appointment time with your disciple. Here are some options:

- Breakfast or lunch
- Before or after a workout or run (perhaps combining with them)
- Before or after church service or organizational meeting
- Before or after a small-group meeting
- Midmorning or midafternoon break time
- Before or after recreational league play
- Before or after a rehearsal
- Following dinner or during midevening
- Before or after a compassionate ministries event

Here are some guidelines:

- Set a time that will be unhurried.
- Determine to meet within time parameters.
- Avoid disrupting family or work schedules.
- Avoid conflicting with church events.
- Send a reminder.
- Pick up the tab (restaurant meetings).
- Make a follow-up contact (e.g., thanks, questions, needs mentioned, or next meeting).

The personal appointment time can be just for building an intentional relationship. It doesn't have to include an agenda, but there are some things that may be included:

- Encouragement
- Praise for efforts
- Progress or needs

71

- Q&A
- Inquiry into personal or family needs
- Church event reminders
- Brief prayer (including prayer requests for others)
- Sharing a Bible verse(s)

4. MAKING THE GOLDEN HOUR GOLDEN

The golden hour is an accumulated 60 minutes of personal contact time with your disciple each week. Whether it may include a 30-minute telephone call, 5 minutes of e-mailing or text messaging or instant messaging, 10 minutes of note card writing, 45 minutes of personal meeting time, or any other combination, the time spent will have an eternal impact. The number of weeks per assignment may be determined by a discipling program in your church, which is a prayerfully planned system of helping the disciple grow in faith.

a. Scaling back or changing directions

When the assignment time has not been predetermined, you might consider some signs that the discipling effort can be scaled back or change directions:

(1) **The disciple is making obvious spiritual progress.**
- Prayer and Bible study have become a part of his or her daily routine.
- The disciple is actively involved in (or leading) a small group.
- The disciple is actively involved in ministry.
- The disciple's lifestyle reflects advancing spiritual maturity.
- The disciple is actively involved in evangelistic outreach.
- The disciple's testimony reflects advanced spiritual growth.
- The disciple is pursuing holiness.

(2) **The relationship has a different dynamic.**
- Personality conflicts indicate the need for reassignment.
- The disciple has become too emotionally dependent on the discipler.
- The disciple's maturity level indicates the need for reassignment (in some cases the disciple may grow *beyond* the experience of the discipler).

(3) **The disciple has reached a "discipler" level.**
- The assignment time has been fulfilled.
- The disciple has indicated a desire to disciple another.
- The disciple is involved in discipleship training.
- The disciple is involved in church planting.

b. Maximizing discipling effectiveness

Paul advised, "Be very careful, then, how you live—not as unwise but as wise, making the most of every opportunity, because the days are evil" (Eph. 5:15-16). The golden hour contact time is filled with *golden minutes*.

(1) **Keep your purpose in mind.**

Hide behind the Cross. Your most important duty is to exalt Christ—not your own efforts.

Keep growing. The holiness lifestyle is one of continual growth. Don't let your ministry busyness detract from your own devotional time. Keep growing in all areas of your Christian life.

(2) **Stay alert.**

The enemy of your personal faith is the enemy of your discipling efforts. Satan will do his best to bring misunderstandings and divisions into play. You will be vulnerable to emotional and physical weariness. Guard your attitudes and actions during those times you feel most vulnerable.

(3) Know your limits.

You won't have the answer for every question. Your advice will be limited to your own learning and experience. Share what you know of God's Word. Share what God has taught you about your faith journey. Avoid anxiety about your abilities or efforts. God knows your heart, and He will use your obedience and faithfulness to impact others.

Introducing others to Jesus Christ and building them in their faith is one of the most rewarding aspects of being a Christian. Remember, the life you influence will influence others—and others. Your work is just the beginning.

⑭ INCORPORATE INTO THE LIFE AND MINISTRIES OF THE CHURCH

New disciples need the life and ministries of a local church (Heb. 10:25). Your task as a discipler also includes incorporating your disciple into the mainstream of a fellowship of believers—whether an established church, church plant, or house church.

(Review chapter 3, "Public Worship.")

How you accomplish that task is a matter of Spirit-led strategy. For some, the mention of "church" may result in interesting responses.

Some have never attended church. The whole concept of a church fellowship isn't relevant to them. Since their families were never encouraged to attend church, they are not familiar with the church's worship traditions. They aren't familiar with the preaching, teaching, Bible study, or music of the local church.

- Speak positively of your own church background.
- Include a study of the church in your discipling.
- Invite them to be your guest for a worship service, followed by a fellowship time.
- Encourage them to take a baptism or new Christian's class.
- Reinforce the importance of making a public declaration of their new faith commitment.
- Reinforce the importance of worshipping with fellow believers, including the reading and study of the Bible in a structured environment.

Some have been turned off by the church. The mention of church brings an unpleasant memory to mind. Perhaps they, or one of their family members, were part of a church split—or some other "church problem." To them, "church" has a negative connotation.

- Listen fairly to their opinions and attitudes of the church.
- Help them understand that the church, like all organizations, has people problems—because it is made up of people.
- Explain that the church has more positive qualities than negative.
- Speak positively of your own church background.
- Reinforce the importance of worshipping with other believers, including the reading and study of the Bible in a structured environment.
- Reinforce the importance of making a public declaration of their new faith commitment.
- Encourage them to take a baptism or new Christian's class.
- Invite them to a worship service as your guest, followed by a fellowship time.
- Introduce them to age-related, positive role models in the church.

Some have abandoned the church. They may have attended church but became disillusioned by a staff member or parishioner or were burned out by overwork and a lack of support. Some may have attended church as children but simply neglected church attendance as they grew older.

- Listen sympathetically to their "story."
- Help them understand that the church, like all organizations, has people problems—because it is made up of people.

- Explain that the church has more positive qualities than negative.
- Speak positively of your own church background.
- Reinforce the importance of worshipping with other believers, including the reading and study of the Bible in a structured environment.
- Reinforce the importance of making a public declaration of their new faith commitment.
- Encourage them to take a baptism or new Christian's class.
- Invite them to a worship service as your guest, followed by a fellowship time.
- Introduce them to age- or interest-related, positive role models in the church.
- Point out positive differences between the contemporary church and the church of their earlier days.
- Reinforce the necessity of ministry as an outworking of their faith.

Each of the "church background" scenarios will present a challenge to the discipler. You will need the wisdom and direction that the Holy Spirit will provide in connecting or reconnecting the disciple to a local church. As James 1:5 says, "If any of you lacks wisdom, he should ask God, who gives generously to all without finding fault, and it will be given to him."

Incorporating the new disciple into the life and ministries of the church can be done at several important "entry points."

1. BAPTISM AND LORD'S SUPPER *(See Chapter 4)*

Observances of the sacraments are opportunities to introduce the new disciple to the life and ministries of the church. For example, as you explain the purpose and ceremony of baptism as a witness to a faith commitment, you will encourage the disciple to use the occasion as a witness to friends and family members. This will not only reinforce the need for baptism as an act of obedience but also introduce the disciple to the importance of outreach and ministry.

- Encourage the disciple to take a baptism or new Christian's class.
- Discuss the biblical reasons for a public witness.
- "Sponsor" the disciple's scheduled baptism (plan a fellowship time, providing refreshments following the baptismal service and child care during and after the ceremony).
- Counsel the disciple in inviting friends and family to the baptism.
- Take digital photos or video of the baptism.
- Ask the presiding minister to reenact the presentation of the baptismal certificate during the fellowship time (for photo opportunity).
- Ask permission to invite a church staff member to attend the fellowship time.

The baptismal service may also be a time of outreach to the disciple's friends and family. Introduce yourself to them and invite them to an upcoming church event or small group. Also, take note of any needs (hospitalization, family death, crisis situations) for further ministry.

The first observance of the Lord's Supper for new disciples is also an opportune time to incorporate them into the life and ministries of the church. They may have received Communion before, but you can now stress the meaning of the event as an act of public witness to their new faith commitment.

- Discuss the meaning of the Lord's Supper observance.
- Sit with the disciple and participate in the observance together.
- Express your thanksgiving to the disciple for his or her new faith commitment.
- Spend time in prayer with the disciple before the observance, asking the Lord to make the service an especially meaningful time.

2. WORSHIP EVENT

A worship event offers a prime opportunity to highlight the disciple's new faith commitment. It provides not only a chance for the disciple to experience worship with a new meaning of its importance but also a choice time for you to introduce the disciple to other believers.

- Discuss the need for public and private worship *(see chapters 2 and 3).*
- Discuss with the disciple (and the pastoral staff, if agreed upon) the possibility of the disciple giving a brief testimony of his or her new faith commitment (counseling him or her about content, time, appearance, and presentation).
- Invite the disciple (along with his or her friends and family) to sit with you during worship.
- Alert greeters or pastoral staff of the disciple's attendance.
- Greet the disciple on arrival.
- Introduce the disciple to other attendees (especially age/interest-related attendees).
- Explain the various segments of the worship time (singing, preaching, teaching, drama, giving, etc.).
- Make sure the disciple has a worship bulletin, church brochure, and so on.
- Assist the disciple with finding child care locations in the building.
- Assist the disciple with attendance registration or visitor signup.
- If appropriate, give the disciple a tour of the facilities (church building site), pointing out the child care, Sunday School classrooms, restrooms, and so on.
- Acquaint the disciple with sermon or study note-taking methods.
- Invite the disciple to dinner or refreshments following the service.

3. SPECIAL EVENT

Special events offer entry points for incorporating disciples into the life and ministries of the church. They may include Christmas and Easter pageants, dinners, church daycare celebrations, auctions, church anniversaries, revivals, missions conventions, and concerts. The discipler should have an action plan for utilizing the event in the discipling process.

- Invite and remind the disciple of the event.
- Explain the purpose of the event, including sending advertising.
- Assist with reservations or tickets.
- Give map directions.
- Inform of child care options.
- Sit with the disciple and friends or family members.
- Share church brochures and information materials.
- Introduce age- or interest-related attendees.
- Accompany the disciple if he or she responds to an altar invitation.
- Encourage invitations to friends and family.
- Provide extra advertising materials.
- Enlist the disciple's assistance with the event or planning.
- Include the disciple in postevent fellowship times.
- Plan a follow-up meeting or fellowship time within two weeks of the event, inviting other attendees, members, and church staff.
- Encourage volunteerism for the next event.

4. SMALL GROUP

Whether a Sunday School class, Bible study, or prayer cell, small groups are an excellent way to include disciples in the church fellowship. The small group becomes a "little church" within a larger church and offers a more personal setting for meeting fellow believers. You may be a small-group teacher or a participant. Either way, make sure your disciple is informed about the group and invited to its meetings. Then use the small-group setting to include the disciple.

- Invite and remind the disciple about the group meeting.
- Explain the purpose of the small group.
- Provide study guides or other materials.
- Make sure the disciple owns a Bible.
- Arrange for child care.
- Introduce the disciple to the group, giving information about his or her interests.
- Sit with the disciple during the group meeting.
- Introduce age- or interest-related attendees.
- Deflect questions that would be uncomfortable for the disciple to answer by redirecting the questions to you or answering them in a generalized way.
- Give the disciple an opportunity to host a small group.
- Encourage volunteerism in setup or teaching (when appropriate).
- Schedule a fellowship time that will include the disciple and other group members.

5. INTEREST GROUP

The different activities of the church are additional entry points for a new disciple. They may include choir or music teams, sports, men's or ladies' fellowships, ongoing Bible studies, youth or young adult ministries. Accompanying the disciple to the interest group may not be practical, but your information and encouragement may help the disciple in joining.

- Provide information about the interest group, including map directions, times, locations, and so on.
- Alert the group leader of your disciple's interests.
- Introduce the disciple to other group members.
- Attend group special events that include your disciple (musicals, drama, sporting events, etc.).
- Commend the disciple on his or her participation and performance.
- Remind the disciple of your prayers regarding his or her participation.

6. MINISTRY TEAM

Once your disciple has completed a basic Bible study or some other new Christian training event, you may want to look for local church ministries that fit your disciple's personality, interests, or abilities and encourage his or her participation. Remembering the "too much too soon" advisory, your relationship with the disciple will give you insights into guiding that person to ministry. Ministry teams (regional, national, or international mission trips; outreach; music or drama; etc.) are "quick study" assignments that give the disciple an awareness of ministry potential and opportunity to minister.

- Pray for your disciple's ministry awareness.
- Provide information on ministry teams.
- Alert ministry team leaders of your disciple's interests and abilities.
- Guide your disciple toward a team.
- Offer to be a prayer partner.
- Help provide sponsorship for team events.

⑮ PRAY DAILY FOR SPIRITUAL GROWTH

Disciples need a support team, behind-the-lines "soldiers" who will do battle with the enemy (Satan) on their behalf. A continual communication in prayer for a prebeliever or believer is a weapon of warfare that can be effective in winning people to Christ and supporting new faith commitments. Paul said, "For we are not fighting against flesh-and-blood enemies, but against evil rulers and authorities of the unseen world, against mighty powers in this dark world, and against evil spirits in the heavenly places" (Eph. 6:12, NLT).

Christian living is a team effort. "Confess your sins to each other and pray for each other so that you may be healed. The prayer of a righteous man is powerful and effective" (James 5:16). Each disciple has a personal responsibility to live in obedience to the Word and will of God, but the "family factor" of Christianity provides additional spiritual protection and strength. First Corinthians 12:12 says, "The body is a unit, though it is made up of many parts; and though all its parts are many, they form one body." Various parts of the physical body support the whole physical body. Likewise, individual members of the "church body" function to support that body.

1. INTERDEPENDENCE

In the letter of Jude the apostle seems to reveal people at various points in their faith journey. But each person—at each point—is dependent on the prayerful concern of other believers:

> Build each other up in your most holy faith, pray in the power of the Holy Spirit, and await the mercy of our Lord Jesus Christ, who will bring you eternal life. In this way, you will keep yourselves safe in God's love. And you must show mercy to those whose faith is wavering. Rescue others by snatching them from the flames of judgment. Show mercy to still others, but do so with great caution, hating the sins that contaminate their lives *(Jude 20-23, NLT)*.

Prayerful concern for another believer is actually a form of spiritual strength training. Notice the disciples' responsibilities to keep themselves "safe in God's love":
- "Build each other up in your most holy faith."
- "Pray in the power of the Holy Spirit."
- "Await the mercy of our Lord Jesus Christ."

Interdependence and mutual ministries are prominent among the responsibilities: "Build each other up." One of the tools for that building is to "pray in the power of the Holy Spirit."

Pray daily for your disciple's spiritual growth:
- Pray for your disciple's faithfulness in private and public worship.
- Pray for your disciple's obedience to the Holy Spirit's guidance.
- Pray for your disciple's Bible study times.
- Pray that your disciple will pursue holiness.
- Pray that your disciple will influence others for Christ.

2. PRAYER PARTNERSHIPS

Two or more believers (including disciplers) may team up to pray for prebelievers or new believers. Their "prayer connection" may mean an *eternal* difference in someone's life. Biblical history proves there is power in partnerships:

- Two brothers were called to be disciples (Matt. 4:18, 21).
- Two disciples were sent to prepare for Jesus' entrance into Jerusalem (Matt. 21:1-3).
- Disciples were sent out to minister two by two (Mark 6:7).
- Seventy disciples were sent out to minister two by two (Luke 10:1).

Jesus also talked about partnership in prayer: "Again I say to you that if two of you agree on earth concerning anything that they ask, it will be done for them by My Father in heaven" (Matt. 18:19, NKJV).

Partnership in prayer is a powerful weapon for spiritual warfare. Prayer partners

- Strengthen individual courage—facing an enemy alone is always more intimidating.
- Help to offset individual weaknesses—for example, one partner may have a stronger gift of faith (1 Cor. 12:9) than the other.
- Keep each other focused—being accountable to another person keeps goals and objectives in mind.
- Remind each other of prayer concerns—one partner may have closer ties to one for whom the partners are praying.
- Widen the area of influence—prayer concern is contagious.

A prayer partnership is not only powerful but also practical. Busy times call for innovative strategies. Arranging for two people to meet in person or online is usually more convenient than bringing a larger group together. Prayer partners may be teamed from within a larger prayer effort (e.g., a prayer cell).

Prayer partnerships may be used *in addition* to individual prayer for your disciple and participation in a combined prayer ministry, such as the prayer cell. They may include your disciple or they may be separate from your discipling meetings.

(1) **What is a prayer partnership?**

A prayer partnership is an agreement between two or more people to pray daily for prebelievers, new believers, or fellow believers (prayer targets) on their prayer list for a specified period of time, in agreement with Matt. 18:19.

(2) **What do prayer partners do?**

Prayer partners pray together either in person, by phone, or by other appropriate means (e.g., video conferencing). They also share victories for answered prayer, motivating them to even bolder prayer advances—breaking down even greater spiritual barriers.

(3) **How should prayer partnerships be formed?**

Prayer partnerships may be formed from an organized prayer effort, such as prayer cells or big brothers/big sister discipling ministries, or may be formed from friendships or staff relationships within the church. When there is a prayer coordinator in the church, the prayer partners will report to the coordinator and receive further instruction about their ministry—along with their prayer list.

(4) **What are the qualifications of a prayer partner?**

Prayer partnerships should be taken seriously. A prayer partner is a committed believer who is pursuing holiness and is active in the ministries of the local church (preferably a member) who has a vision for prayer. Praying for prebelievers and other believers is an intensive responsibility. The most vivid example is Jesus' prayer in the Garden of Gethsemane prior to His crucifixion.

> Then Jesus went with his disciples to a place called Gethsemane, and he said to them, "Sit here while I go over there and pray." He took Peter and the two sons of Zebedee along with him, and he began to be sorrowful and troubled. Then he said to them, "My soul is overwhelmed with sorrow to the point of death. Stay here and keep watch with me." Going a little

79

farther, he fell with his face to the ground and prayed, "My Father, if it is possible, may this cup be taken from me. Yet not as I will, but as you will" *(Matt. 26:36-39).*

Other guidelines for prayer partnerships may include the following:

- Partners should complete a basic Bible study or discipleship course.
- Partners should be trained.
- Partners should be active in the church (preferably members).
- Partners should be active in the outreach of the church (including the big brothers/big sisters or prayer cells).
- Partners should be of the same gender (unless spouse partnership).
- Partners should be disciples who have a solid witness.
- Partners should not reveal confidential prayer concerns.
- Partners should be disciples known for their faithfulness.
- Partners should be of the same age range.

(5) When and where should prayer partners meet?

Prayer partners should plan to meet at least once each week to pray for their prayer list and prayer concerns. The meetings may be in person, by phone, or by some other media (e.g., video conferencing). They may even be held before or after a church service or event.

- Meetings should not interfere with church schedules.
- Meetings should not interrupt family times or work schedules.
- Meetings should focus on prayer for prayer list members (prayer targets), not just on conversations about other interests.
- Meetings should not include gossip about other believers or about church matters.

Generally, in-person prayer meetings should not be held in private locations away from public access. Others (including family, prayer coordinator, or staff) should be made aware of in-person meeting times.

Online meetings may also have guidelines:

- Messages should be brief and to the point.
- Pass-along attachments (e.g., political, humorous, controversial, cultural) should be avoided.
- Online addresses should not be shared without permission.
- Copies to other online users should be avoided (especially if it concerns a confidential prayer concern).
- Messages should always reflect positively on the church or church staff.

(6) What should be included in prayer partner meetings?

Though prayer times will vary in length and content depending on the experience of the prayer partners, they may include

- Sharing Bible promises about prayer or faith
- Sharing prayer concerns from the prayer list
- Taking turns praying for the concerns
- Mutually encouraging comments
- Praying for the other prayer partner
- Praising God for answered prayer

(7) Who should the prayer partners pray for?

Primarily, your prayer partnership is focused on the needs of your disciple. Other prayer list names may be provided by the prayer coordinator, a pastoral staff member, or from big brother/big sister ministries or prayer cells. Those names will be people who are prebelievers, new believers, or believers with a spiritual need. Additional names may be added through prayer requests from the congregation or supplied personally. Their names will be added to a prayer partner prayer list and assigned to a prayer partnership.

(8) How long should a prayer partnership last?

Your partnership may focus on the length of discipling time with your disciple. The length of other prayer partnerships will vary. Some will remain prayer partners for a long period of time, while others will form a prayer partnership for an immediate or short-term need. It may be helpful to begin with a designated length of time. For example, a prayer partnership may be established for a yearly assignment. The length of time will depend on such factors as

- The compatibility of the prayer partners
- The urgency of the need
- The support of staff, friends, or family
- The answer to a prayer concern

Prayer partners should establish some boundaries from the beginning in order to be able to dissolve the partnership amicably if needed. The partners should also be informed at the outset that new partnerships may be formed.

(9) How can prayer partnerships be multiplied?

As answers to prayer are announced to the prayer partners and to the congregation (including answered prayer from your own discipling effort), enthusiasm will begin to build for prayer partnerships. Testimonies of new faith commitments may be part of a public worship service. Also, prayer partner testimonies of how God has blessed the partnership may be included. An ongoing prayer partner ministry can be enhanced in several ways:

(a) Announce that new prayer partnerships will soon be formed

- Launch a three- to four-week message series or short-term class on prayer.
- Include Bible verses on prayer and faith in printed publications or electronic announcements.
- Announce answers to prayer in worship services or small-group meetings.
- Include video clips on prayer in worship services.
- Place signage that includes Bible verses or quotes about prayer in high traffic areas of the church or meeting place.
- Have one or more prayer partners write a 50- to 100-word article on what prayer partnerships have meant to them (letting them know in advance that the article may be edited for word count and content).
- Have one or more persons who have been on the prayer list and have made new faith commitments write a 50- to 100-word article on how they have benefited from the prayer partnerships (letting them know in advance that the article may be edited for word count and content).

(b) Organize a one-session prayer partnerships training class

- Have current prayer partners pray in advance for the success of the training.
- Assign a class leader/teacher (usually the prayer coordinator).
- Reserve a classroom or meeting place.
- Announce a post-service or -event meeting and a location.
- Distribute the duties of a prayer partner handout.
- Distribute a signup card to those interested.
- Announce a class date, time, and location.
- Assign room preparation.

- Compile teaching materials.

(c) Conduct the prayer partnerships class (120 minutes)

- Session 1: How to Pray for Others (intercessory prayer) (30 minutes)
- Break (10 minutes)
- Session 2: The Duties of a Prayer Partner (amplified lesson from the "Duties of a Prayer Partner" handout) (30 minutes)
- Form Prayer Partnerships (20 minutes)
  - Ask for volunteer partnerships.
  - Appoint partnerships.
  - Have the prayer partners meet for brief prayer time.

(d) Introduce prayer partners in a worship service or meeting

- Present diploma for class completion.
- Have congregation members submit prayer requests on prayer request cards.
- Announce that prayer partners will pray for requests submitted to the pastoral staff or prayer coordinator.

(e) Compile and assign prayer requests in a post-service or –event meeting

- Compile duplicate lists on prayer list cards.
- Place the prayer list cards in church stationery envelopes.
- Distribute envelopes to prayer partnerships.
- Give encouragement and instruction.
- Close in prayer.

Praying for your disciples individually or in a prayer partnership is a powerful way to help them stay on track. Let them know that there are others who are praying for them. Encourage them to submit prayer requests as the needs arise.

Remember the words of Jesus to His disciple: "I have prayed for you . . . that your faith may not fail" (Luke 22:32).

🔟 LOOK FOR SPIRITUAL GIFTS

Who knows what your disciple may become! A pastor? A missionary? A church planter? A denominational leader? A local church leader? An influential layperson? God knows! The seeds of greatness have already been planted in every child of God. Their abilities and personalities are part of His master design that benefits the Kingdom:

> It was he who gave some to be apostles, some to be prophets, some to be evangelists, and some to be pastors and teachers, to prepare God's people for works of service, so that the body of Christ may be built up until we all reach unity in the faith and in the knowledge of the Son of God and become mature, attaining to the whole measure of the fullness of Christ. Then we will no longer be infants, tossed back and forth by the waves, and blown here and there by every wind of teaching and by the cunning and craftiness of men in their deceitful scheming. Instead, speaking the truth in love, we will in all things grow up into him who is the Head, that is, Christ. From him the whole body, joined and held together by every supporting ligament, grows and builds itself up in love, as each part does its work *(Eph. 4:11-16)*.

Your task as a discipler is to help disciples discover and utilize their spiritual gifts. It is also your task to teach them how the Holy Spirit enables and empowers them to use their gift through sanctification, through being filled with the Holy Spirit (Acts 1:8). Their "complete surrender" to God unleashes God's "complete supply" to them. Personalities and abilities surrendered fully to Jesus Christ become the channels through which He reaches the lost and strengthens His Church. Your insights into spiritual gifts will help you guide disciples into their individual ministries.

1. WHAT ARE THE DIFFERENCES BETWEEN THE *FRUIT* OF THE SPIRIT AND THE *GIFTS* OF THE SPIRIT?

Fruit	Gifts
1. Defines what a Christian is	1. Determines what a Christian does
2. Same in every Christian	2. Different in each Christian
3. Singular	3. Plural
4. Satan cannot imitate	4. Satan can imitate
5. Deals with character	5. Deals with service ministry
6. End in itself	6. Means to an end
7. Permanent/eternal	7. Will cease
8. According to spirituality and maturity	8. Not according to spirituality

2. WHAT IS A SPIRITUAL GIFT?

"It was he who gave some to be apostles, some to be prophets, some to be evangelists, and some to be pastors and teachers" (v. 11).

A spiritual gift is a divinely enabled ability that is intended to be used in fulfilling the mission of Christ through the local church. H. Orton Wiley wrote:

The gifts of the Spirit are known in Scripture as *charismata* . . . or gifts of grace. Hence there is an internal connection between the graces and the gifts in the administration of the Spirit. The gifts are the divinely ordained means and powers with which Christ endows His Church in order to enable it to properly perform its task on earth.[12]

Those gifts include not only "up-front, platform" gifts but also "behind-the-scenes, support" gifts. There are a wide variety of gifts that, used corporately, can be of great strength and influence. Believers should seek to discover what Spirit-enabled abilities they may possess. How?

- Identify interests that support Christ's mission.
- Identify natural talents that would fulfill that interest.
- Reflect on how those interests and talents may be used for Christ.
- Look for opportunities to utilize interests and talents in mission supporting efforts.

Remember in seeking spiritual gifts that the greatest gift is the Spirit *himself.* "The Holy Spirit whom the Father will send at my request, will make everything plain to you. He will remind you of all the things I have told you. I'm leaving you well and whole. That's my parting gift to you" (John 14:25-26, TM). His sanctifying and empowering presence was promised by Christ and fulfilled at Pentecost (Acts 2:15-17).

3. TO WHOM ARE SPIRITUAL GIFTS GIVEN?

Spiritual gifts are given to followers of Jesus Christ.

- "Each one should use whatever gift he has received to serve others, faithfully administering God's grace in its various forms" (1 Pet. 4:10).
- "Now to each one the manifestation of the Spirit is given for the common good" (1 Cor. 12:7).

In one sense, those gifts are "activated" or "released" when a person makes a faith commitment to Christ and is spiritually reborn (1 Cor. 12:13). The Holy Spirit, the giver of spiritual gifts, indwells the new believer: "Repent and be baptized, every one of you, in the name of Jesus Christ for the forgiveness of your sins. And you will receive the gift of the Holy Spirit" (Acts 2:38). The believer who responds obediently to His inner promptings (through the Bible and through a conscience enlightened by the Bible) will seek to be led by Him in helping to accomplish Christ's Great Commission (Matt. 28:18-20).

Believers do not "choose" their gifts. They are given to them by Christ in accordance with His will:

- "All these are the work of one and the same Spirit, and he gives them to each one, just as he determines" (1 Cor. 12:11).
- "God has arranged the parts in the body, every one of them, just as he wanted them to be" (1 Cor. 12:18).

Spiritual gifts work together in harmony through believers—each gift complimenting the gift(s) of another. No one believer has all of the spiritual gifts, nor is any one gift common to all (1 Cor. 12:12-18).

4. WHAT IS THE PURPOSE OF SPIRITUAL GIFTS?

Spiritual gifts serve a heavenly purpose. Though the gifts are given to people in an earthly setting, they help to fulfill the broader, eternal scope of God's promises of forgiveness, holiness, and life beyond the grave.

a. They qualify

"To prepare God's people for works of service" (Eph. 4:12*a*).

Spiritual gifts are "credentials" for the building of God's kingdom on earth (Acts 2). They also are "tools" used to

- Communicate the good news of the gospel to prebelievers
- Encourage and enlighten believers by the Word of God
- Organize the church into a functioning body
- Enlist the church in accomplishing growth

b. They edify

"So that the body of Christ may be built up" (Eph. 4:12b).

The use of spiritual gifts is like physical fitness training. Weights and motion and attitude combine in a decided effort to tone and strengthen the body. Muscles of the body react to physical exercise and grow as a result.

When believers make conscious and obedient use of their spiritual gifts, they help to build up the Body, the Church. Paul said, "Therefore, my dear friends, as you have always obeyed—not only in my presence, but now much more in my absence—continue to work out your salvation with fear and trembling, for it is God who works in you to will and to act according to his good purpose" (Phil. 2:12-13).

c. They unify

"Until we all reach unity in the faith and in the knowledge of the Son of God" (Eph. 4:13a).

If you have ever watched a rowing team, you know how important it is for every member of the team to work in coordination with the other team members. One person going his or her own way can result in the team's failing to reach the finish line—or the boat to overturn. Spiritual gifts are codependent; they must be exercised with unity in mind. And they must have a goal. For the believer, the goal is to *know* Christ, be more *like* Christ, and to *share* Christ.

d. They fortify

"Become mature, attaining to the whole measure of the fullness of Christ" (Eph. 4:13b).

Packaged food comes with a label that identifies "Nutrition Facts." The facts identify not only vitamin percentage values but also calorie and fat content. Thus the protein and fat content affect the "daily value" of the food. Spiritual gifts add "daily value" for the well-being of the body and its individual members. They may differ in "percentage values" according to the maturity level of the believer, but they fortify—they produce nutrients for body growth.

e. They exemplify

"Then we will no longer be infants, tossed back and forth by the waves, and blown here and there by every wind of teaching and by the cunning and craftiness of men in their deceitful scheming. Instead, speaking the truth in love, we will in all things grow up into him who is the Head, that is, Christ" (vv. 14-15).

True disciples are known for several important qualities that identify them as followers of Jesus Christ:

- They publicly declare their faith.
- They live by the principles of the Word of God.
- They respond to the needs of others.
- They serve the Lord through the church.
- They support fellow believers.
- They practice public and private worship.
- They have a vision to reach the lost in other nations.
- They cheerfully give of their time, talent, and treasure to advance the kingdom of God.

85

The use of spiritual gifts gives the believer an opportunity to put God's grace "on display." "But God had mercy on me so that Christ Jesus could use me as a prime example of his great patience with even the worst sinners. Then others will realize that they, too, can believe in him and receive eternal life" (1 Tim. 1:16, NLT).

f. They glorify

"From him the whole body, joined and held together by every supporting ligament, grows and builds itself up in love, as each part does its work" (Eph. 4:16).

The use of spiritual gifts brings honor to God's creative power and purpose in Christ, His only Son:

He is the image of the invisible God, the firstborn over all creation. For by him all things were created: things in heaven and on earth, visible and invisible, whether thrones or powers or rulers or authorities; all things were created by him and for him. He is before all things, and in him all things hold together *(Col. 1:15-17)*.

They also reflect on the power of His salvation. The new direction, interest, and effort of the believer using spiritual gifts is proof of his or her new creation in Christ (2 Cor. 5:17).

5. HOW DO *HUMAN TALENTS* AND SPIRITUAL *GIFTS* DIFFER?

Your abilities are the raw materials that God blesses and empowers to accomplish His eternal purpose. Distributed and anointed by the Holy Spirit, they are made alive through their dedication to Christ and His cause.

- One spiritual gift is not more important than another; and all are used for the same purpose.
- They are not to be used as personal attention-getters.
- They are to be used to bring attention to Christ.
- They should not be a source of contention between believers; they should be a source of unity.

How do human talents and spiritual gifts differ? Notice:

Talents	Gifts
1. Inherited from forefathers	1. Given by the Holy Spirit
2. Present from natural birth	2. Present from new birth
3. God-given to all members of the human race	3. God-given too members of Christ's body
4. For human activities	4. For ministry of the Body
5. Can be operated independently of the Holy Spirit	5. Dependent on the Holy Spirit
6. Ministers primarily on a natural level	6. Ministers on a spiritual level
7. Effects are usually temporal/finite	7. Effects are eternal/infinite
8. Glorifies self	8. Glorifies God

6. DISCOVERING SPIRITUAL GIFTS

Helping disciples discover abilities that may be used in Kingdom building is essential not only to their spiritual growth but also to the spiritual, financial, organizational, and numerical growth of the church.

- Introduce them to a spiritual gifts survey.
- Point out the abilities that could be used in the church.
- Make their discovery of their spiritual gifts a matter of mutual prayer.
- Help them see how a Spirit-filled life will bring wholeness—and holiness—to their spiritual journey.

⑰ ENLIST IN MINISTRY

Author John Mason said, "Too many people make cemeteries of their lives by burying their talents and gifts. These abilities are like deposits in our personal accounts, and we get to determine the interest. The more . . . attention we give them, the more valuable they become."[13]

Jesus talked about "the revelations," the display of God's graces:

> You are the light of the world—like a city on a hilltop that cannot be hidden. No one lights a lamp and then puts it under a basket. Instead, a lamp is placed on a stand, where it gives light to everyone in the house. In the same way, let your good deeds shine out for all to see, so that everyone will praise your heavenly Father *(Matt. 5:14-16, NLT)*.

Nowhere does the "light" of a disciple's life bring a warmer and brighter glow than through the ministries of the church.

> All of you together are Christ's body, and each of you is a part of it. Here are some of the parts God has appointed for the church:
>
> first are apostles,
>
> second are prophets,
>
> third are teachers,
>
> then those who do miracles,
>
> those who have the gift of healing,
>
> those who can help others,
>
> those who have the gift of leadership,
>
> those who speak in unknown languages.

Are we all apostles? Are we all prophets? Are we all teachers? Do we all have the power to do miracles? Do we all have the gift of healing? Do we all have the ability to speak in unknown languages? Do we all have the ability to interpret unknown languages? Of course not! So you should earnestly desire the most helpful gifts *(1 Cor. 12:27-31, NLT)*.

Your disciples must understand how important they are to the ongoing impact of the church on society. Again it was said of the Early Church, "These who have turned the world upside down have come here too" (Acts 17:6, NKJV). Your disciples are "difference makers." They use the gifts God the Holy Spirit released in their lives when they were saved and empowered when they were sanctified.

You are the coach-encourager who will teach your disciples how to take an active part in church ministry

- Through training
- Through internship with another
- Through appointment to a specific position
- Through discipling another
- Through prayer ministries
- Through small groups

Not only will you encourage them to find a place of ministry, but you will also guide them in enlisting in that ministry—always in cooperation with the leadership of the church.

1. LOCAL CHURCH MINISTRY

Most outside observers of the local church have no idea of the depth of cooperation needed to fulfill the church's mission and purpose. To them, church involvement means attending services. Those within the church know that it involves far more. They know that the church is "organizational machinery" that needs both parts and labor. The "parts" make the machinery run, while the "labor" keeps it running! And the Holy Spirit's presence and power keeps it fueled and lubricated.

Opportunities for ministry in the local church are many—and varied. There is a place for your disciple's interest and ability. For example:

- Teaching
- Small groups
- Prayer
- Building maintenance and repair
- Vehicle maintenance and repair
- Child care
- Youth ministry
- Young adult ministry
- Senior adult ministry and elder care
- Music
- Drama
- Staging and costuming
- Outreach
- Accounting
- Office assistance
- Design and publishing
- Technical support (computers, sound, lighting, taping)
- Construction
- Publicity
- Sign painting
- Decorating
- Cooking
- Hosting
- Ushering and greeting
- Security and safety
- Retailing
- Transportation
- Distribution

Again, not all spiritual gifts will include platform, stage, or classroom presentations. Behind the scenes, support ministries are vital to the church's public ministry. Whether using the gifts of helps, administration, teaching, preaching, or evangelism, believers of most age-groups can be plugged in to the ministry of the local church.

Encourage their enlistment in local church ministry:

- List the types of ministries.
- Consult with local church leadership about needed volunteers.
- Ask local church leadership to supply job descriptions for volunteer needs.

- Evaluate your disciple's ability and experience.
- Match abilities and experience with volunteer needs.
- Approach your disciple with volunteer possibilities.
- Recommend a volunteer position.
- Introduce the disciple to the administrator needing volunteers.
- Advise the disciple of your prayers and wisdom in assisting him or her with a volunteer position.
- Advise the disciple of next-level ministries (small-group leadership, ministerial training, and church planting).

2. MISSIONS MINISTRY

The church also has a global mission—and consequently is in need of disciples who will assist with that mission (Luke 10:1-2). Your spiritual mentoring can encourage disciples to have a "global vision."

- Teach them about Christ's global commission.
- Share missions publications with them.
- Invite them to assist with a missions convention.
- Tell them how your missions involvement has benefited you.
- Encourage them to participate in a missions trip.
- Encourage correspondence for or with overseas missionaries.
- Encourage them to be prayer partners with an overseas missionary.
- Encourage them to support a mission or missionary.
- Inform them of denominational missions opportunities.
- Teach them about next-level missions ministries (short-term or vocational missions opportunities).

3. COMPASSIONATE MINISTRY

Disciples must understand that their own community is a mission field. A global vision for missions begins with a vision to minister to people in their immediate area. Enlisting them in compassionate ministries is a great place to start. Compassionate ministries are, in a biblical sense, holistic. That is, they minister to the whole person—spiritually, physically, emotionally, socially, and financially.

- Worship services
- Bible studies
- Food distribution
- Clothing distribution
- Evangelism and discipleship
- Health training
- Crisis pregnancy
- Counseling services
- Legal services
- Financial management training
- Child care
- Elder care
- Recreation

89

- Camping
- Job training
- Skills training
- Women's shelters
- Homeless care
- Parenting training
- Medical clinics
- ELL (English language learners) classes
- Housing
- Transportation services
- Referrals to community services

A disciple's experience with compassionate ministries may be just the beginning of a wider ministry—including vocational ministry. You can encourage disciples to become involved in compassionate ministry:

- Study compassionate ministries in the Scriptures (e.g., the Good Samaritan or first-century church).
- Acquaint them with ministry opportunities in the community.
- Ask them to help you with a compassionate ministry on-site.
- Introduce them to community compassionate ministries leaders.
- Inform them of denominational compassionate ministries.

4. SMALL-GROUP MINISTRY

Small groups, such as neighborhood Bible studies, big brothers/big sisters, or prayer cells is an exciting introduction to ministry. Enlisting disciples in an organized small group—or launching one—will give them the experience and responsibility for various ministries. Small groups are good training grounds:

- The "audience" is smaller in number.
- It demands hands-on participation.
- Material costs are fewer.
- Group members may be friends or associates.
- Leadership skills are developed.
- People skills are developed.

Working in a small-group setting usually builds self-confidence. And the training and supervision that are usually offered provides a support system. Your church may provide one or more small-group ministries (including Sunday School and Vacation Bible School). As a discipler, you can encourage volunteerism in small groups as a way of enriching Bible study skills and using spiritual gifts.

5. EVENT MINISTRY

Special events offer both the discipler and the disciple a time of training and hands-on experience. A church-wide or community-wide event, such as a crusade, concert, film showing, or nationally known speaker, demands dedicated and trained support workers.

- Publicity
- Setup
- Ushering

- Technical support
- Product table assistance
- Counseling
- Literature distribution
- Parking
- Child care
- Follow-up
- Planning
- Committee leadership

Disciples not only will see ministry in action but also will most likely receive training that will help them in their spiritual growth.

- Check the church or community calendar for events.
- Inform disciples of event ministry opportunities.
- Assist them with contacting event organizers.
- If possible, join them in volunteering for the event.
- Partner with them in prayer for the event.
- Review soul-winning and discipleship training techniques.

Remember Barnabas? His little-known efforts to introduce Saul (later Paul) to the "way" resulted in a ministry that reaches into eternity. Billions of people have heard the gospel as a result of his faithful ministry. A spiritually blind man received sight. A spiritually troubled man received peace and purpose. A forgiven man received a lifelong direction.

Your commitment to D-I-S-C-I-P-L-E has no boundaries, because the Christ you serve has no limits!

"Go and make disciples."

SECTION THREE
APPENDIXES

APPENDIX A

EACH ONE DISCIPLE ONE CHECKLIST

☐ Begin to prepare a series of messages concerning the responsibility to make and mature disciples. (A list of passages on discipleship is found in Appendix C.)

☐ Prepare worship folder inserts, newsletter articles, posters, drama, and PowerPoint presentations. (If you have access to video production, use this medium as well.)

☐ Begin planning and developing strategy and leadership for a service of dedication.

☐ Each One Disciple One begins with a service of dedication.

☐ Prepare and develop messages with an emphasis on our responsibility to make and mature disciples.

☐ Have posters ready for Each One Disciple One to be displayed at the service of dedication.

☐ Challenge every member of the congregation to

    1. Win one person to Christ during the year

    2. Pray that God will help him or her win one person

    3. Disciple the new Christians

    4. Prepare them for baptism

    5. Encourage them to become members of the church

    6. Disciple them to become soul winners

    7. Encourage them to participate in the miracle of multiplication by discipling Christians newer than themselves

APPENDIX B

SERMON OUTLINE: A MODEL FOR DISCIPLESHIP

Introduction: Jesus Trained His Disciples in Phases.

A. The Invitation to Come and See! (John 1:39)

B. The Invitation to Come and Follow Me! (Mark 1:16-20)

C. The Invitation to Come and Be with Him! (Mark 3:13-14)

D. The Invitation to Remain in Him! (John 15:7-8)

Conclusion: He Called Them to a Vision and Not a Job!

APPENDIX C

THE MAKING OF A DISCIPLE

Disciple-Making Scriptures

Matthew 28:18-20
John 20:21
Mark 16:15-18
Luke 24:44-49
Acts 1:8
John 15:7-17
Luke 14:25-35

Luke 9:23-25
Luke 6:40
2 Timothy 3:17
Matthew 9:36-38
John 1:39
Mark 1:16-20
Mark 3:13-14

Definition of a Disciple

Luke 9:23-25
John 8:31
John 13:34-35

Luke 14:25-35
Matthew 9:36-38
John 15:7-17

APPENDIX D

MY COMMITMENT TO GROW IN CHRIST CHECKLIST

- ☐ I will become a growing Christian in prayer, accountability, reading the Word, and in witnessing.
- ☐ I will become involved in a small-group discipling class.
- ☐ I will prepare and study materials in a small-group discipling class.
- ☐ I will be involved in a committed devotional life.
- ☐ I will put myself under the leadership of a small-group leader.
- ☐ I will memorize at least 30 scripture verses per year.
- ☐ I will write out and share my personal testimony.
- ☐ I will cultivate friendships with the unchurched.
- ☐ I will involve myself in outreach events.
- ☐ I will seek a place of service in the local church.
- ☐ I will seek to disciple another Christian.

Signed _____ Date _____

APPENDIX E

BECOMING A DISCIPLE
(Leader's Guide)

1

Pursuing Holiness
(Leader's Guide)

Introduction

    a. Every successful person sets <u>goals</u>.

    b. It's the same in your <u>spiritual</u> journey with God.

1. Growing

    You keep <u>going</u> by <u>growing</u> (2 Pet. 3:18).

2. Learning

    How do you grow in knowledge? You <u>discipline</u> yourself to <u>study</u> and to put into <u>practice</u> what you learn from <u>His Word</u> (2 Tim. 2:15).

3. Perfecting

    "No one serving as a soldier gets involved in civilian affairs—he wants to please his commanding officer. Similarly, if anyone competes as an athlete, he does not receive the victor's crown unless he competes according to the rules. The hardworking farmer should be the first to receive a share of the crops" (2 Tim. 2:4-6).

    a. Each of the illustrations used by the apostle—the <u>soldier</u>, the <u>athlete</u>, and the <u>farmer</u>—describes someone who has a great amount of <u>focus</u>, <u>dedication</u>, and <u>determination</u>. They "<u>pursue perfection</u>."

    b. That doesn't mean they are perfect in all of their <u>actions</u>; it simply means that they are "perfect" in their <u>direction</u> and in their <u>intention</u>.

    c. What is your <u>goal</u>? God has already spelled it out in the Bible: "But just as he who called you <u>is holy</u>, so <u>be holy</u> in <u>all you do</u>; for it is written: 'Be holy, because I am holy'" (1 Pet. 1:15-16).

4. Dedication

    a. God wants you to be spiritually <u>complete</u>.

    b. You are called to be like Him in your <u>attitude</u> and <u>actions</u>.

    c. You are a follower of <u>Christ</u>—a Christian (Christ-one, one of Christ's), one who seeks to be like <u>Him</u> in everything you do. You are His "<u>disciple</u>" (learner, follower). You are dedicated to <u>obeying Him</u> and learning how to be <u>like Him</u>.

    d. Dedication is a mark of <u>excellence</u>.
- Discipline your <u>mind</u> to learn everything you can about Christ and <u>the Bible</u>.
- You can copy Him in your <u>love</u> and <u>service</u> to others.
- You can "line up" your heart with the <u>principles</u> He taught and "aim" to live by them.
- You can determine to live by the <u>rules</u> written in the Bible.
- You can pursue <u>holiness</u>.

5. Assurance

a. What is involved in that pursuit?

Be certain of your <u>salvation</u>.

- When you received Christ into your heart as an act of faith, you were <u>saved</u> from being <u>lost</u> (Titus 3:5-7).
- You were <u>away</u> from God, your <u>sin</u> (breaking His law on purpose: "Everyone who sins breaks the law; in fact, sin is lawlessness" [1 John 3:4]) had <u>separated</u> you from Him.
- Breaking the law meant paying the <u>penalty</u>: "The wages of sin is <u>death</u>" (Rom. 6:23a).
- You deserved the "wage" (penalty) of (spiritual) <u>death</u>.
- But God loved you so much He provided a <u>way back</u> to Him.
- He paid the <u>price</u> for your salvation from being lost by offering His only Son, Jesus, as your <u>representative</u>: "The gift of God is eternal life in Christ Jesus our Lord" (Rom. 6:23b).
- At the moment you told God how sorry you were for disobeying His will and His Word (you <u>repented</u>), and asked Jesus Christ to come <u>into your life</u>, and to be the Lord of your life.
- Every act of <u>disobedience</u> was <u>forgiven</u>—and <u>forgotten</u>: "I will forgive their wickedness and will remember their sins no more" (Heb. 8:12).

b. There are several "<u>signs</u>" that give you the <u>assurance</u> that you have been found—that you have been saved from being lost.
- *God's promise* (John 1:12)
- *The Holy Spirit's witness* (Rom. 8:16)
- *Fruit of the Spirit* (Gal. 5:22-23)
- *Change of direction* (2 Cor. 5:17)
- *Desire for service* (Matt. 9:35-38)
- *Hunger for holiness* (1 Pet. 1:13-16). As you continue to <u>pursue</u> holiness, you will discover <u>areas of your life</u> that you can turn over to Him. You will even come to a point where you will <u>make a decision</u> to turn every area of your life over to Him (called sanctification—being "set apart" for holy use).

6. Reaching

a. As a Christian you have a goal God has given you. You are to <u>pursue holiness</u>.

b. By faith you invited Jesus to <u>come into</u> your life. And by faith you can ask Him to <u>take full control of</u> your life.

2

Private Worship
(Leader's Guide)

Introduction

a. "Time-out" is a <u>disciplined</u> act of <u>stopping</u> what you are doing and <u>focusing</u> on something else.

b. Every disciple needs a time of <u>private worship</u>—away from the <u>busyness</u> or the <u>noise</u> of the day.

c. There are five key ingredients in a daily time of private worship:

1. Prayer

a. What is prayer?

(Prayer is a communications <u>link</u> between <u>people</u> and <u>God</u>. Prayer expresses your <u>love</u> for God and your <u>dependence</u> on Him to supply your daily <u>needs</u>—physical, spiritual, social, financial, and emotional.)

    (1) Prayer is <u>talking</u> to God (Heb. 4:16).

    (2) Prayer is <u>responding</u> to God (Deut. 6:3).

        (a) He speaks to you through the <u>Bible</u> (Ps. 119:105).

        (b) He speaks to you <u>inwardly</u> (John 16:13).

        (c) He speaks to you through the counsel of <u>other Christians</u> (Prov. 10:21).

        (d) He speaks to you through <u>circumstances</u> (Rom. 8:28).

b. Why should I pray?

    (1) You pray to express a <u>need</u> (John 16:23*b*-24).

    (2) You pray for forgiveness of <u>sin</u> (1 John 1:9).

    (3) You pray for <u>healing</u> (James 5:14-15).

    (4) You pray for the <u>needs</u> of others (Phil. 1:4).

    (5) You pray for the <u>increase</u> of God's kingdom (John 14:6).

    (6) You pray for community and national <u>leaders</u> (1 Tim. 2:1-2).

c. When should I pray?

Considerations:
* Are you a morning person or a night person?
* What part of the day seems to be less <u>hectic</u>?
* When will you be <u>less interrupted</u> by the schedules of others in the home?

d. Where should you pray?

It should be a place where you can focus on being <u>alone with God</u> (John 6:14-15).

e. How should I pray?

* Prayer is a natural <u>conversation</u>.
* There are no <u>required</u> words.
* Jesus gave us an <u>example</u> in Matt. 6:9-14.

From those verses, one of the most familiar prayers, the Lord's Prayer, was formed, and an outline of that prayer will give you a prayer pattern.

    (1) "Our Father, who art in heaven, hallowed be Thy name."

Begin your prayer by <u>praising</u> God, thanking Him for <u>who He is</u>, as revealed in the Bible, and for <u>what He has done</u> for you today or in the past (days, weeks, months).

    (2) "Thy Kingdom come, Thy will be done, on earth as it is in heaven."

Pray for God's will to be done in <u>your life</u> and in the <u>world</u> (in your home, in your place of employment, in the lives of your family, in your church; and in your nation and in the lives of its leaders).

(3) **"Give us this day our daily bread."**

Present your daily <u>needs</u> to God (called petition) and ask Him to meet them individually—spiritual, physical, financial, family—according to <u>His will</u>; present your needs for the day and the <u>needs of others</u> (called intercession).

(4) **"Forgive us our trespasses, as we forgive those who trespass against us."**

Ask God to forgive any willful (on purpose) <u>sin</u> in your life. Also, ask God to forgive any <u>deeds or actions</u> committed by others toward you.

(5) **"Lead us not into temptation, but deliver us from evil."**

Pray for God's <u>power</u> and <u>wisdom</u> to help you face areas where you are spiritually vulnerable (temptations).

(6) **"Thine is the kingdom, the power and the glory, forever and ever. Amen."**

Praise God that He is in control of <u>your life</u> and in control of <u>everything around you</u>. Thank Him for being <u>faithful</u> to you; for loving you and forgiving you.

2. Bible Reading

a. What is the Bible?

(1) The Bible (meaning "book") is a <u>library</u>.

(2) It contains <u>66</u> different "books" and letters, written under the inspiration of the <u>Holy Spirit</u> by over <u>40</u> authors, during a span of <u>1,600</u> years.

(3) It is divided into two sections: the <u>Old</u> Testament and the <u>New</u> Testament.

b. Why read the Bible?

(2 Tim. 3:16-17)

(1) **Because it is the <u>inspired</u> Word of God.** ("Inspired" means "God-breathed." God the Holy Spirit "breathed" His message into the minds and hearts of those who wrote it down and translated it for our understanding.)

(2) **Because it teaches us basic <u>doctrines</u> (beliefs).**

(a) God's Word, the Bible, is true (Ps. 119:160).

(b) It addresses at least three important areas:
- Where we came from (<u>creation</u>)
- Why we are here (<u>purpose</u>)
- Where we are going after we die (<u>eternity</u>)

(3) **Because it teaches us how to <u>live</u>.** (We need the directions.)

(4) **Because it gives us a sense of <u>belonging</u>** (1 John 5:19-20).

(5) **Because it tells how to serve God.**

c. How to read the Bible

- Read it with <u>anticipation</u> that God will reveal His eternal love for you in the words you will read. Pray before you read.
- Read it with an <u>open mind</u>. Be willing to accept its truth.
- Read it with an <u>eagerness</u> to do what it says to do—and be what it says to be.
- Read it <u>with a system</u>. (e.g., Read through the Bible, one book at a time, over the course of a year. Study each chapter of the book. Then, look at each verse of the chapter.)

3. Include a Devotional Book

4. Meditation

Think on a verse of <u>Scripture</u>—letting God's Word "soak into your inner person" like water soaks the soil.

5. Praise

What is praise?

(1) Praise is <u>reflecting</u> on God's character, goodness, and faithfulness.

(2) It expresses <u>out loud</u> what you feel inside.

(3) It expresses <u>your gratitude</u> to Him for what He has done for you.

(4) Your "format" of praise may vary:
- Listening to <u>Christian music</u>
- <u>Singing a song</u>
- <u>Meditating</u> on God's goodness
- <u>Reading</u> hymns or songs

3

Public Worship
(Leader's Guide)

Introduction

a. Christians need <u>each other</u>.

b. Private worship is important, but it is also important to worship with other followers of Jesus Christ in a <u>church setting</u>.

c. The Scriptures almost always speak of believers in a <u>group setting</u> (Heb. 10:25). Public worship is vital to your spiritual growth.

d. In the New Testament, the word translated "church" is found over 100 times. And in over 90 of those instances the word refers to a group of Christians in a <u>particular location</u>—in other words, "local churches."

e. In the beginnings of the Church era, the disciples of Jesus Christ either <u>found a place of public worship</u> when they arrived in a place or they <u>started one</u>. It should be the same today.

f. Christian churches were formed to provide a place to meet the spiritual needs of their attendees.

1. The Importance of the Church

You need the church.

a. You need the <u>nourishment</u> of the church.

   (1) You need its Bible <u>messages</u> and <u>teaching</u>.

   (2) You need its <u>fellowship</u> and <u>counsel</u>.

b. You need the <u>guidance</u> of the church.

   (1) As a river needs banks to channel its energy and direction, you need the "banks" of a local church for <u>spiritual energy</u> and <u>direction</u> (Heb. 13:17).

   (2) The prayerful concern of fellow believers in the local church setting may keep you from making the wrong <u>life decisions</u>.

c. You need the <u>ministry</u> of the church.

Vocational and lay ministers in the local church have been gifted to <u>care for you</u> spiritually (Eph. 4:7, 11-13).

d. You need the <u>activities</u> of the church.

e. You need the <u>fellowship</u> of the church.

You need the <u>friendship</u> of other Christians.

f. You need the <u>administration</u> of the church.

   (1) You are a <u>steward</u> (manager) of God's <u>resources</u> (Ps. 24:1).

   (2) You have a responsibility to use those resources <u>wisely</u>.

   (3) The administration of the local church gives you opportunity to use your <u>time</u>, <u>treasures</u>, and <u>talents</u> in a resourceful way.

2. The Worship of the Church

• God <u>inhabits</u> the worship of His people.

• When you meet together with other spiritual seekers you are being <u>strengthened</u> by their strength.

• Worship is putting <u>words</u> and <u>actions</u> to your <u>thanksgiving</u> for God's goodness.

• Public worship is a time to <u>actively express</u> your <u>love</u> for God.

a. *Singing*

b. *Serving*

c. *Giving*

d. *Sharing*

e. *Learning:* The local church is a place where Christians not only meet to praise God but also <u>learn more about Him</u>. It is a learning center through its

    (1) <u>Programs</u> of Christian education

    (2) <u>Classes</u>, including Sunday School and small-group Bible studies

    (3) <u>Sermons and lessons</u>

As you wholeheartedly <u>contribute</u> positively and openly to the <u>parts</u> of worship—and keep focused on <u>Jesus Christ</u>, not on the attitudes or actions of others—<u>worship</u> will be an experience that brings <u>wholeness</u> to your entire week.

4

Observing the Sacraments
(Leader's Guide)

Introduction

    a. Sacraments are <u>ceremonies</u>, instituted by <u>Christ</u>, to <u>remind</u> His followers of <u>important moments</u> in their own spiritual journey.

    b. Christ asked His disciples to remember <u>two</u> important events: His <u>baptism</u> and the <u>Lord's Supper</u> (also known as the Eucharist, meaning thanksgiving).

        (1) The first, His baptism, was the occasion when His <u>Heavenly Father announced His approval</u> of the life and mission of Jesus, His only Son, <u>prior</u> to the start of His <u>earthly ministry</u> (Matt. 3:16-17).

        (2) The second occasion was the Lord's Supper—the time when He had a <u>meal with His disciples</u> just <u>prior</u> to His <u>crucifixion</u>. During that meal He revealed to them the events of His death and its importance to His followers (Matt. 26:26-28).

    c. Most Christians observe these two sacraments, baptism and the Lord's Supper, during <u>public worship</u> services on a regular basis.

1. Baptism

    a. The importance of baptism

        (1) Jesus referred to baptism as an identifying mark of <u>discipleship</u> (Mark 16:16).

        (2) Jesus also included the observance of baptism <u>in His commission</u> to the disciples to spread the good news of the Kingdom (Matt. 28:19).

        (3) Just as the <u>ceremonial washings</u> in the Old Testament symbolized cleansing of sin, so also did <u>baptism</u> in the New Testament.

    b. The purpose of baptism

        (1) Baptism by immersion symbolizes the <u>death</u> (into the water) and <u>resurrection</u> (out of the water) of Jesus Christ—and the candidate's <u>identifying</u> with them.

        (2) Baptism also signifies the candidate's "death" to the <u>old life of rebellion</u> against God and "life" to the new one of <u>obedience and faith</u> in Christ (Col. 2:12).

        (3) The ceremony of baptism does not make you a <u>child of God</u>. You are a child of God <u>through faith</u> in the Lord Jesus Christ. Baptism is a <u>sign</u> of that commitment to Christ.

    c. The witness of baptism

Baptism not only <u>affirms</u> the candidate's <u>relationship</u> with God through <u>faith</u> in Jesus Christ but also testifies <u>to others</u> about that relationship.

2. The Lord's Supper

    • Observing the Lord's Supper (also known as Communion) was a practice of <u>New Testament</u> Christians.

    • Their <u>obedience</u> to the Master <u>in observing</u> the Lord's Supper became a <u>pattern</u> for all Christians (1 Cor. 11:23-26).

    a. The elements

        (1) The bread symbolizes the <u>body of Jesus Christ</u>, which was offered and broken on the Cross of Calvary.

        (2) The wine (substituted with grape juice in most Protestant churches) represents the <u>blood of Christ</u>, which was shed on that Cross.

(3) When you observe Communion you are <u>remembering</u>—and giving praise for—the <u>total commitment</u> that Jesus Christ made for your <u>salvation</u>.

(4) The sacraments are called <u>means of grace</u>; that is, God uses them to <u>communicate</u> His presence and His blessings.

b. *Preparing for the Lord's Supper*

(1) Those who observe Communion should do so <u>in faith</u>. Participating in the Lord's Supper is an act that <u>testifies</u> of our complete trust in the sacrifice of Christ and that He is the only hope for salvation from being lost (Acts 4:12).

(2) Those who observe Communion should do so <u>in harmony</u> with God. Any <u>unconfessed sin</u> should be repented of.

(3) Third, those who observe Communion should do so in harmony <u>with others</u> (Matt. 5:23-24).

5

Witnessing
(Leader's Guide)

Introduction

    a. Witnessing is in the "job description" of <u>every</u> follower of Jesus Christ (Luke 24:46-48).

    b. The news is too good to <u>keep to yourself</u>: "For God so <u>loved</u> the world that he <u>gave</u> his one and only Son, that whoever <u>believes</u> in him shall <u>not perish</u> but have <u>eternal life</u>" (John 3:16).

1. Witnessing Principles

    Witnessing is <u>sharing</u> your <u>faith</u>. (You tell others what Jesus did for you.)

    a. Witnessing is giving a "<u>firsthand account</u>" of your life-changing relationship with God.

    b. God trusts you to be a part of making a <u>positive influence</u> throughout the earth.

    c. Jesus <u>promised</u> He would be there with you.

2. Witnessing Plans

    Acts 1:8: "You will receive power when the Holy Spirit comes on you; and you will be my witnesses in Jerusalem, and in all Judea and Samaria, and to the ends of the earth." (Each of the areas mentioned are places where you can be a witness.)

    a. "Jerusalem": <u>local</u>
Your first "mission field" is in your own <u>community</u>.
- <u>Family</u>
- <u>Church</u>
- <u>Job</u> (being careful not to use company time)
- <u>School</u> (being careful not to use school time)

    (1) **Start with your <u>testimony</u>.**
        (a) What my life was like <u>before</u> Jesus Christ
        (b) How I came to <u>know</u> Him
        (c) How my life has <u>changed</u> since He is in it

    (2) **Learn a presentation <u>plan</u>.**
        A<u>dmit</u> that you have sinned (Rom. 3:23).
        B<u>elieve</u> that Jesus Christ died for you (John 1:12).
        C<u>onfess</u> that Jesus Christ is Lord of your life (Rom. 10:9-10).
        Dear Lord Jesus, I know that I am a sinner. I believe that You died for my sins and arose from the grave. I now turn from my sins and invite You to come into my heart and life. I receive You as my personal Savior and follow You as my Lord. Amen.

    (3) **Gather resource materials** (immediate <u>follow-up</u>).
        (a) <u>Bible</u> (Mark the verses that outline the plan.)
        (b) <u>Literature</u> (Printed presentations of the gospel.)
        (c) <u>Books or booklets</u> (Christian literature.)

    b. "Judea": <u>regional</u>
Establish your own ministry or participate in one already established by your church.
- Volunteer to be a sponsor or counselor in a <u>camping</u> ministry.
- Join (or form) a <u>music</u> ministry or drama group for itinerant ministries.
- Assist with the <u>planting</u> of a new church.
- Volunteer to help in a <u>compassionate</u> relief effort.

- Sponsor a local or regional church ministry.

c. *"Ends of the earth": global*

(1) Followers of Jesus Christ are called to a global mission (Matt. 24:14).

(2) You are an important part of that global strategy:
- Pray for missions and missionaries.
- Give toward missions interests.
- Sign up for an overseas missions trip if possible.
- Communicate encouragement to missionaries.
- Learn about mission fields and missionaries.
- Help others understand the importance of missions.

6

Discipling Other Believers
(Leader's Guide)

Introduction

    a. Discipling is <u>building up</u> other believers in <u>their faith</u>.

    b. The highest level of discipling was that of <u>Christ's</u> (Matt. 10:2).

1. He <u>Prayed</u> for Them

    To one apostle He said, "I have prayed for you, Simon, that <u>your faith may not fail</u>" (Luke 22:32).

        (1) He knew how the devil would try to <u>destroy</u> the apostles' faith.

        (2) He knew that the busyness of life would often <u>distract</u> them.

        (3) He knew there would be temptations to go with the <u>crowd</u> instead of standing alone for the right. So He <u>prayed</u>.

2. He <u>Ministered</u> to Them

    a. Jesus taught the greatest truths in the <u>simplest</u> way.

    b. Jesus met them <u>where they were</u>.

        (1) They (your disciples) may need to know very <u>basic beliefs</u>.

        (2) Your <u>patience</u> in teaching them at their level of <u>understanding</u> will be of great value.

3. He <u>Encouraged</u> Them

    a. He didn't hide the <u>hardships</u>, but He gave them <u>hope</u> as well.

    b. They must know that they are on the winning side; they must know that Jesus forever won the victory for them on the Cross (John 19:30).

      • Lead them to the <u>promises</u> of God's Word.

      • Lead them to the <u>prophecies</u> of God's Word.

      • Lead them to the <u>priorities</u> of God's Word.

4. He <u>Spent Time</u> with Them

    (Mark 6:30-32)

        (1) Jesus wanted them to know that discipleship wasn't all about <u>work</u>.

        (2) They needed times of <u>relaxation</u>.

5. He <u>Taught</u> Them

    a. Some of the best teachings the apostles received were <u>on the job</u>.

    b. Situations would arise that gave Jesus an opportunity <u>to apply spiritual truth</u> to the incident (Mark 8:14-15).

    c. Your discipleship will not just be focused on a study. It will include <u>lessons from life</u>.

6. He <u>Corrected</u> Them

    a. There will be times when you will have to correct your disciple about <u>attitudes</u> or <u>actions</u> that are contrary to <u>God's Word</u> (Matt. 8:23-26).

    b. Lovingly and carefully point out the difference between a <u>worldview</u> and a <u>Christ-view</u>.

7. He **Defended** Them

    a. Jesus often came to the defense of His followers (Mark 2:18-20).

    b. Let those you disciple know that you will stand by them—even when others may stand against them.
- <u>Send them</u> an encouraging e-mail or note.
- <u>Call them</u> when you hear of difficult times in their lives.
- Constantly <u>remind them</u> of your availability and interest.
- <u>Share</u> some promises from the Bible.

8. He **Challenged** Them

    a. Jesus didn't call His apostles to a life of <u>ease</u>; He called them to a life of challenge (Mark 6:7-11).

    b. Don't be afraid to <u>challenge</u> your disciples. Set some goals and objectives.
- Assign a Bible reading or a prayer time.
- Set some evangelism goals.
- Draw up a prayer list of their friends or associates who need to know Christ as Savior and then commit to praying for those same people.

9. He **Trusted** Them

Jesus gave the greatest work of all to 12 people who didn't have any previous <u>experience</u>.

    (1) He called them and <u>trained</u> them,

    (2) He assigned and <u>encouraged</u> them, and

    (3) He sent them and <u>inquired</u> of them (Matt. 10:1).

111

7

Stewardship
(Leader's Guide)

Introduction

a. The Bible says, "It is required in stewards that one be found <u>faithful</u>" (1 Cor. 4:2, NKJV).

b. A steward <u>manages</u> the assets of another (God is not only the Creator of the world but also the Owner) (Ps. 24:1).

c. Stewardship involves the <u>wise use</u> of our <u>time</u>, our <u>talent</u>, and our <u>treasure</u>.

d. We will have to give an answer for the way we used <u>God's resources</u>.

e. Areas of stewardship:

1. Time

a. Because of <u>sin's influence</u>, the opportunity to use time for selfish and worldly endeavors will always be present.

b. Christians are called to "<u>redeem</u>" the time—to <u>reclaim it</u>—and to put it to use for the <u>pursuit of holiness</u>, personally and in the faith community.

c. Give <u>honor</u> and <u>thanksgiving</u> to God in giving back a portion of <u>your time</u> to Him.

2. Talent

a. Each person is given an <u>ability</u> that can be used to glorify God (1 Cor. 12:4-7).

b. You are practicing <u>stewardship</u> when you use your talent in supporting and building God's kingdom.

c. Sharing your talent is a way to express your <u>faithfulness</u> to the Lord Jesus Christ—in His church.

3. Treasure

a. God has established a <u>standard</u> for Christian giving. It's called a "<u>tithe</u>."

b. Tithe means "<u>tenth</u>" (Mal. 3:10).

c. Jesus <u>taught</u> the practice of giving the "tenth" in New Testament times (Matt. 23:23).

d. Tithing (giving a tenth) is the <u>fairest</u> standard for giving possible. (The person who <u>earned little</u> is instructed to give the same percentage as the person who <u>earned more</u>. And both were given the same <u>promise</u>.) (Mal. 3:10).

e. The giving of our treasure to the Lord is just as important as the giving of our <u>time and talents</u>.

f. Tithing is not a duty; it is a <u>delight</u> (2 Cor. 9:7).

g. You can start tithing by <u>putting aside</u> a tenth of your income and giving it through the <u>local church</u>. (But for the disciples who are serious about their spiritual journey, giving a tithe is just the beginning. They may want to give an <u>offering</u> above their tithe.)

8

Church Membership
(Leader's Guide)

Introduction

 a. When you became a <u>follower of Jesus Christ</u>, you became a part of the family of God (John 1:12).

 b. Commitment to an organized unit of that family (the local church)—including identifying with its <u>core beliefs</u>, participating in its <u>ministries</u>, and cooperating in its <u>leadership</u>—is a <u>disciplined</u> step.

1. Church Membership Is an Opportunity to Defend the Church

 a. The Church (all believers in Christ) is <u>under attack</u> by its enemies.

 b. There are those who would seek to <u>destroy it</u> from within. Being a Christ-centered, Christ-directed member of the church is an <u>opportunity</u> to help keep it on course.

2. Church Membership Is an Opportunity to Align with the Church's <u>Beliefs</u>

 a. The local church is founded on <u>biblical beliefs</u> (doctrines) of the Bible.

 b. By joining with it, you help to defend its <u>core values</u>.

3. Church Membership Is an Opportunity to Develop <u>Leadership</u> Skills

 a. Churches also offer leadership training. That training not only could help you in church ministry but also could make you more effective in <u>other areas of life</u>.

 b. Membership introduces you to the largest—and usually the most loyal—<u>leadership segment</u> of the local church (Acts 2:42).

4. Church Membership Is an Opportunity to Add Strength to the Church's <u>Outreach</u>

 a. The local church's mission is to reach unbelievers with the gospel of Jesus Christ, lead them into a relationship with Jesus Christ, and then build them up in the faith.

 b. It also has a mandate to plant other churches. You can be a part of that exciting effort.

5. Church Membership Is an Opportunity to Have a <u>Voice</u> in the Church's Direction

Your input could be one that will help the local church decide on a <u>biblical purpose</u>.

6. Church Membership Is an Opportunity to Help <u>Determine a Church's Leadership</u>

You have an opportunity to prayerfully influence the <u>purpose</u> and <u>mission</u> of the local church's leadership team.

7. Church Membership Is an Opportunity to <u>Influence</u> Your Family

Church membership has a <u>loyalty</u> factor.

8. Church Membership Is an Opportunity to Influence Other <u>Believers</u>

Finding a church and joining it is <u>an example</u> to other believers.

9. Church Membership Is an Opportunity to Be a Part of the Church's <u>Ministry Team</u>

You will soon discover places within the organization where you can plug in your <u>talents and interests</u>.

10. Church Membership Is an Opportunity to Help Guide the Church's <u>Stewardship</u> Decisions

a. The church organization, as well as its members, should be careful to use God's resources in a way that brings <u>glory to Him</u>.

b. Your financial interest in its ministry will give you the joy of seeing the <u>positive results</u>.

APPENDIX F

BECOMING A DISCIPLE
(Student's Guide)

1

Pursuing Holiness
(Student's Guide)

Introduction

a. Every successful person sets _____.

b. It's the same in your _____ journey with God.

1. Growing

You keep _____ by _____ (2 Pet. 3:18).

2. Learning

How do you grow in knowledge? You _____ yourself to _____ and to put into _____ what you learn from _____ (2 Tim. 2:15).

3. Perfecting

"No one serving as a soldier gets involved in civilian affairs—he wants to please his commanding officer. Similarly, if anyone competes as an athlete, he does not receive the victor's crown unless he competes according to the rules. The hardworking farmer should be the first to receive a share of the crops" (2 Tim. 2:4-6).

a. Each of the illustrations used by the apostle—the _____, the _____, and the _____—describes someone who has a great amount of _____, _____, and _____. They "_____ _____."

b. That doesn't mean they are perfect in all of their _____; it simply means that they are "perfect" in their _____ and in their _____.

c. What is your _____? God has already spelled it out in the Bible: "But just as he who called you _____, so _____ in _____; for it is written: 'Be holy, because I am holy'" (1 Pet. 1:15-16).

4. Dedication

a. God wants you to be spiritually _____.

b. You are called to be like Him in your _____ and _____.

c. You are a follower of _____—a Christian (Christ-one, one of Christ's), one who seeks to be like _____ in everything you do. You are His "_____" (learner, follower). You are dedicated to _____ and learning how to be _____.

d. Dedication is a mark of _____.
  • Discipline your _____ to learn everything you can about Christ and _____.
  • You can copy Him in your _____ and _____ to others.

- You can "line up" your heart with the _____ He taught and "aim" to live by them.
- You can determine to live by the _____ written in the Bible.
- You can pursue _____.

5. Assurance

a. What is involved in that pursuit?

Be certain of your _____.

- When you received Christ into your heart as an act of faith, you were _____ from being _____ (Titus 3:5-7).
- You were _____ from God, your _____ (breaking His law on purpose: "Everyone who sins breaks the law; in fact, sin is lawlessness" [1 John 3:4]) had _____ you from Him.
- Breaking the law meant paying the _____: "The wages of sin is _____" (Rom. 6:23a).
- You deserved the "wage" (penalty) of (spiritual) _____.
- But God loved you so much He provided a _____ to Him.
- He paid the _____ for your salvation from being lost by offering His only Son, Jesus, as your _____: "The gift of God is eternal life in Christ Jesus our Lord" (Rom. 6:23b).
- At the moment you told God how sorry you were for disobeying His will and His Word (you _____), and asked Jesus Christ to come _____ _____, and to be the Lord of your life.
- Every act of _____ was _____—and _____: "I will forgive their wickedness and will remember their sins no more" (Heb. 8:12).

b. There are several "_____" that give you the _____ that you have been found—that you have been saved from being lost.

- *God's promise* (John 1:12)
- *The Holy Spirit's witness* (Rom. 8:16)
- *Fruit of the Spirit* (Gal. 5:22-23)
- *Change of direction* (2 Cor. 5:17)
- *Desire for service* (Matt. 9:35-38)
- *Hunger for holiness* (1 Pet. 1:13-16). As you continue to _____ holiness, you will discover _____ that you can turn over to Him. You will even come to a point where you will _____ to turn every area of your life over to Him (called sanctification—being "set apart" for holy use).

6. Reaching

a. As a Christian you have a goal God has given you. You are to _____.

b. By faith you invited Jesus to _____ your life. And by faith you can ask Him to _____ your life.

2

Private Worship
(Student's Guide)

Introduction

    a. "Time-out" is a _____ act of _____ what you are doing and _____ on something else.

    b. Every disciple needs a time of _____—away from the _____ or the _____ of the day.

    c. There are five key ingredients in a daily time of private worship:

1. Prayer

    a. What is prayer?
(Prayer is a communications _____ between _____ and _____. Prayer expresses your _____ for God and your _____ on Him to supply your daily _____—physical, spiritual, social, financial, and emotional.)

        (1) **Prayer is _____ to God** (Heb. 4:16).

        (2) **Prayer is _____ to God** (Deut. 6:3).

           (a) He speaks to you through the _____ (Ps. 119:105).

           (b) He speaks to you _____ (John 16:13).

           (c) He speaks to you through the counsel of _____ (Prov. 10:21).

           (d) He speaks to you through _____ (Rom. 8:28).

    b. Why should I pray?

        (1) **You pray to express a _____** (John 16:23*b*-24).

        (2) **You pray for forgiveness of _____** (1 John 1:9).

        (3) **You pray for _____** (James 5:14-15).

        (4) **You pray for the _____ of others** (Phil. 1:4).

        (5) **You pray for the _____ of God's kingdom** (John 14:6).

        (6) **You pray for community and national _____** (1 Tim. 2:1-2).

    c. When should I pray?

    Considerations:
    • Are you a morning person or a night person?
    • What part of the day seems to be less _____?
    • When will you be _____ by the schedules of others in the home?

    d. Where should you pray?
It should be a place where you can focus on being _____ (John 6:14-15).

    e. How should I pray?
    • Prayer is a natural _____.
    • There are no _____ words.
    • Jesus gave us an _____ in Matt. 6:9-14.
From those verses, one of the most familiar prayers, the Lord's Prayer, was formed, and an outline of that prayer will give you a prayer pattern.
    (1) **"Our Father, who art in heaven, hallowed be Thy name."**
Begin your prayer by _____ God, thanking Him for _____, as re-

vealed in the Bible, and for _____ for you today or in the past (days, weeks, months).

(2) "Thy Kingdom come, Thy will be done, on earth as it is in heaven."

Pray for God's will to be done in _____ and in the _____ (in your home, in your place of employment, in the lives of your family, in your church; and in your nation and in the lives of its leaders).

(3) "Give us this day our daily bread."

Present your daily _____ to God (called petition) and ask Him to meet them individually—spiritual, physical, financial, family—according to _____; present your needs for the day and the _____ (called intercession).

(4) "Forgive us our trespasses, as we forgive those who trespass against us."

Ask God to forgive any willful (on purpose) _____ in your life. Also, ask God to forgive any _____ committed by others toward you.

(5) "Lead us not into temptation, but deliver us from evil."

Pray for God's _____ and _____ to help you face areas where you are spiritually vulnerable (temptations).

(6) "Thine is the kingdom, the power and the glory, forever and ever. Amen."

Praise God that He is in control of _____ and in control of _____ _____. Thank Him for being _____ to you; for loving you and forgiving you.

2. Bible Reading

a. *What is the Bible?*

(1) The Bible (meaning "book") is a _____.

(2) It contains _____ different "books" and letters, written under the inspiration of the _____ by over _____ authors, during a span of _____ years.

(3) It is divided into two sections: the _____ Testament and the _____ Testament.

b. *Why read the Bible?*

(2 Tim. 3:16-17)

(1) Because it is the _____ Word of God. ("Inspired" means "God-breathed." God the Holy Spirit "breathed" His message into the minds and hearts of those who wrote it down and translated it for our understanding.)

(2) Because it teaches us basic _____ (beliefs).
(a) God's Word, the Bible, is true (Ps. 119:160).
(b) It addresses at least three important areas:
- Where we came from (_____)
- Why we are here (_____)
- Where we are going after we die (_____)

(3) Because it teaches us how to _____. (We need the directions.)

(4) Because it gives us a sense of _____ (1 John 5:19-20).

(5) Because it tells how to serve God.

c. *How to read the Bible*

- Read it with _____ that God will reveal His eternal love for you in the words you will read. Pray before you read.
- Read it with an _____. Be willing to accept its truth.
- Read it with an _____ to do what it says to do—and be what it says to be.
- Read it _____. (e.g., Read through the Bible, one book at a time, over the course of a year. Study each chapter of the book. Then, look at each verse of the chapter.)

3. Include a Devotional Book

4. Meditation

Think on a verse of _____—letting God's Word "soak into your inner person" like water soaks the soil.

5. Praise

What is praise?

(1) Praise is _____ on God's character, goodness, and faithfulness.

(2) It expresses _____ what you feel inside.

(3) It expresses _____ to Him for what He has done for you.

(4) Your "format" of praise may vary:
- Listening to _____
- _____
- _____ on God's goodness
- _____ hymns or songs

3

Public Worship
(Student's Guide)

Introduction

    a. Christians need _____.

    b. Private worship is important, but it is also important to worship with other followers of Jesus Christ in a _____.

    c. The Scriptures almost always speak of believers in a _____ (Heb. 10:25). Public worship is vital to your spiritual growth.

    d. In the New Testament, the word translated "church" is found over 100 times. And in over 90 of those instances the word refers to a group of Christians in a _____ _____—in other words, "local churches."

    e. In the beginnings of the Church era, the disciples of Jesus Christ either _____ _____ when they arrived in a place or they _____. It should be the same today.

    f. Christian churches were formed to provide a place to meet the spiritual needs of their attendees.

1. The Importance of the Church

You need the church.

    a. You need the _____ of the church.

        (1) You need its Bible _____ and _____.

        (2) You need its _____ and _____.

    b. You need the _____ of the church.

        (1) As a river needs banks to channel its energy and direction, you need the "banks" of a local church for _____ and _____ (Heb. 13:17).

        (2) The prayerful concern of fellow believers in the local church setting may keep you from making the wrong _____.

    c. You need the _____ of the church.

Vocational and lay ministers in the local church have been gifted to _____ spiritually (Eph. 4:7, 11-13).

    d. You need the _____ of the church.

    e. You need the _____ of the church.

You need the _____ of other Christians.

    f. You need the _____ of the church.

        (1) You are a _____ (manager) of God's _____ (Ps. 24:1).

        (2) You have a responsibility to use those resources _____.

        (3) The administration of the local church gives you opportunity to use your _____, _____, and _____ in a resourceful way.

2. The Worship of the Church

    • God _____ the worship of His people.

    • When you meet together with other spiritual seekers you are being _____ by their strength.

- Worship is putting _____ and _____ to your _____ for God's goodness.
- Public worship is a time to _____ your _____ for God.

a. *Singing*

b. *Serving*

c. *Giving*

d. *Sharing*

e. *Learning:* The local church is a place where Christians not only meet to praise God but also _____. It is a learning center through its

    (1) _____ of Christian education

    (2) _____, including Sunday School and small-group Bible studies

    (3) _____

As you wholeheartedly _____ positively and openly to the _____ of worship—and keep focused on _____, not on the attitudes or actions of others— _____ will be an experience that brings _____ to your entire week.

4

Observing the Sacraments
(Student's Guide)

Introduction

a. Sacraments are _____, instituted by _____, to _____ His followers of _____ in their own spiritual journey.

b. Christ asked His disciples to remember _____ important events: His _____ and the _____ (also known as the Eucharist, meaning thanksgiving).

    (1) The first, His baptism, was the occasion when His _____ _____ of the life and mission of Jesus, His only Son, _____ to the start of His _____ (Matt. 3:16-17).

    (2) The second occasion was the Lord's Supper—the time when He had a _____ _____ just _____ to His _____. During that meal He revealed to them the events of His death and its importance to His followers (Matt. 26:26-28).

c. Most Christians observe these two sacraments, baptism and the Lord's Supper, during _____ services on a regular basis.

1. Baptism

a. The importance of baptism

    (1) Jesus referred to baptism as an identifying mark of _____ (Mark 16:16).

    (2) Jesus also included the observance of baptism _____ to the disciples to spread the good news of the Kingdom (Matt. 28:19).

    (3) Just as the _____ in the Old Testament symbolized cleansing of sin, so also did _____ in the New Testament.

b. The purpose of baptism

    (1) Baptism by immersion symbolizes the _____ (into the water) and _____ (out of the water) of Jesus Christ—and the candidate's _____ with them.

    (2) Baptism also signifies the candidate's "death" to the _____ _____ against God and "life" to the new one of _____ in Christ (Col. 2:12).

    (3) The ceremony of baptism does not make you a _____. You are a child of God _____ in the Lord Jesus Christ. Baptism is a _____ of that commitment to Christ.

c. The witness of baptism

Baptism not only _____ the candidate's _____ with God through _____ in Jesus Christ but also testifies _____ about that relationship.

2. The Lord's Supper

    • Observing the Lord's Supper (also known as Communion) was a practice of _____ Christians.

    • Their _____ to the Master _____ the Lord's Supper became a _____ for all Christians (1 Cor. 11:23-26).

a. The elements

(1) The bread symbolizes the _____, which was of-fered and broken on the Cross of Calvary.

(2) The wine (substituted with grape juice in most Protestant churches) represents the _____, which was shed on that Cross.

(3) When you observe Communion you are _____—and giving praise for—the _____ that Jesus Christ made for your _____.

(4) The sacraments are called _____; that is, God uses them to _____ His presence and His blessings.

b. Preparing for the Lord's Supper

(1) Those who observe Communion should do so _____. Participating in the Lord's Supper is an act that _____ of our complete trust in the sacrifice of Christ and that He is the only hope for salvation from being lost (Acts 4:12).

(2) Those who observe Communion should do so _____ with God. Any _____ should be repented of.

(3) Third, those who observe Communion should do so in harmony _____ (Matt. 5:23-24).

5

Witnessing
(Student's Guide)

Introduction

 a. Witnessing is in the "job description" of _____ follower of Jesus Christ (Luke 24:46-48).

 b. The news is too good to _____: "For God so _____ the world that he _____ his one and only Son, that whoever _____ in him shall _____ but have _____" (John 3:16).

1. Witnessing Principles

 Witnessing is _____ your _____. (You tell others what Jesus did for you.)

 a. Witnessing is giving a "_____" of your life-changing relationship with God.

 b. God trusts you to be a part of making a _____ throughout the earth.

 c. Jesus _____ He would be there with you.

2. Witnessing Plans

 Acts 1:8: "You will receive power when the Holy Spirit comes on you; and you will be my witnesses in Jerusalem, and in all Judea and Samaria, and to the ends of the earth." (Each of the areas mentioned are places where you can be a witness.)

 a. *"Jerusalem":* _____
 Your first "mission field" is in your own _____.
- _____
- _____
- _____ (being careful not to use company time)
- _____ (being careful not to use school time)

 (1) **Start with your** _____.
  (a) What my life was like _____ Jesus Christ
  (b) How I came to _____ Him
  (c) How my life has _____ since He is in it

 (2) **Learn a presentation** _____.
  A_____ that you have sinned (Rom. 3:23).
  B_____ that Jesus Christ died for you (John 1:12).
  C_____ that Jesus Christ is Lord of your life (Rom. 10:9-10).
  Dear Lord Jesus, I know that I am a sinner. I believe that You died for my sins and arose from the grave. I now turn from my sins and invite You to come into my heart and life. I receive You as my personal Savior and follow You as my Lord. Amen.

 (3) **Gather resource materials** (immediate _____).
  (a) _____ (Mark the verses that outline the plan.)
  (b) _____ (Printed presentations of the gospel.)
  (c) _____ (Christian literature.)

 b. *"Judea":* _____
 Establish your own ministry or participate in one already established by your church.
- Volunteer to be a sponsor or counselor in a _____ ministry.
- Join (or form) a _____ ministry or drama group for itinerant ministries.
- Assist with the _____ of a new church.
- Volunteer to help in a _____ relief effort.
- _____ a local or regional church ministry.

c. *"Ends of the earth":* _____
   (1) Followers of Jesus Christ are called to a global _____ (Matt. 24:14).
   (2) _____ are an important part of that global strategy:
   - _____ for missions and missionaries.
   - _____ toward missions interests.
   - _____ for an overseas missions trip if possible.
   - _____ encouragement to missionaries.
   - _____ about mission fields and missionaries.
   - _____ others understand the importance of missions.

6

Discipling Other Believers
(Student's Guide)

Introduction

  a. Discipling is _____ other believers in _____.

  b. The highest level of discipling was that of _____ (Matt. 10:2).

1. He _____ for Them

  To one apostle He said, "I have prayed for you, Simon, that _____

  _____" (Luke 22:32).

   (1) He knew how the devil would try to _____ the apostles' faith.

   (2) He knew that the busyness of life would often _____ them.

   (3) He knew there would be temptations to go with the _____ instead of standing alone for the right. So He _____.

2. He _____ to Them

  a. Jesus taught the greatest truths in the _____ way.

  b. Jesus met them _____.

   (1) They (your disciples) may need to know very _____.

   (2) Your _____ in teaching them at their level of _____ will be of great value.

3. He _____ Them

  a. He didn't hide the _____, but He gave them _____ as well.

  b. They must know that they are on the winning side; they must know that Jesus forever won the victory for them on the Cross (John 19:30).
   • Lead them to the _____ of God's Word.
   • Lead them to the _____ of God's Word.
   • Lead them to the _____ of God's Word.

4. He _____ with Them

  (Mark 6:30-32)

   (1) Jesus wanted them to know that discipleship wasn't all about _____.

   (2) They needed times of _____.

5. He _____ Them

  a. Some of the best teachings the apostles received were _____.

  b. Situations would arise that gave Jesus an opportunity _____

  _____ to the incident (Mark 8:14-15).

  c. Your discipleship will not just be focused on a study. It will include _____

  _____.

6. He _____ Them

  a. There will be times when you will have to correct your disciple about _____ or

  _____ that are contrary to _____ (Matt. 8:23-26).

b. Lovingly and carefully point out the difference between a _____ and a
    _____.

7. He _____ Them

a. Jesus often came to the defense of His followers (Mark 2:18-20).

b. Let those you disciple know that you will stand by them—even when others may stand against
    them.
    • _____ an encouraging e-mail or note.
    • _____ when you hear of difficult times in their lives.
    • Constantly _____ of your availability and interest.
    • _____ some promises from the Bible.

8. He _____ Them

a. Jesus didn't call His apostles to a life of _____; He called them to a life of challenge (Mark 6:7-
    11).

b. Don't be afraid to _____ your disciples. Set some goals and objectives.
    • Assign a Bible reading or a prayer time.
    • Set some evangelism goals.
    • Draw up a prayer list of their friends or associates who need to know Christ as Savior and then
      commit to praying for those same people.

9. He _____ Them

Jesus gave the greatest work of all to 12 people who didn't have any previous
_____.

    (1) He called them and _____ them,
    (2) He assigned and _____ them, and
    (3) He sent them and _____ of them (Matt. 10:1).

7

Stewardship
(Student's Guide)

Introduction

a. The Bible says, "It is required in stewards that one be found _____" (1 Cor. 4:2, NKJV).

b. A steward _____ the assets of another (God is not only the Creator of the world but also the Owner) (Ps. 24:1).

c. Stewardship involves the _____ of our _____, our _____, and our _____.

d. We will have to give an answer for the way we used _____.

e. Areas of stewardship:

1. T_____

a. Because of _____, the opportunity to use time for selfish and worldly endeavors will always be present.

b. Christians are called to "_____" the time—to _____—and to put it to use for the _____, personally and in the faith community.

c. Give _____ and _____ to God in giving back a portion of _____ to Him.

2. T_____

a. Each person is given an _____ that can be used to glorify God (1 Cor. 12:4-7).

b. You are practicing _____ when you use your talent in supporting and building God's kingdom.

c. Sharing your talent is a way to express your _____ to the Lord Jesus Christ—in His church.

3. T_____

a. God has established a _____ for Christian giving. It's called a "_____."

b. Tithe means "_____" (Mal. 3:10).

c. Jesus _____ the practice of giving the "tenth" in New Testament times (Matt. 23:23).

d. Tithing (giving a tenth) is the _____ standard for giving possible. (The person who _____ is instructed to give the same percentage as the person who _____. And both were given the same _____.) (Mal. 3:10).

e. The giving of our treasure to the Lord is just as important as the giving of our _____.

f. Tithing is not a duty; it is a _____ (2 Cor. 9:7).

g. You can start tithing by _____ a tenth of your income and giving it through the _____. (But for the disciples who are serious about their spiritual journey, giving a tithe is just the beginning. They may want to give an _____ above their tithe.)

8

Church Membership
(Student's Guide)

Introduction

   a. When you became a _____ , you became a
part of the family of God (John 1:12).

   b. Commitment to an organized unit of that family (the local church)—including identifying with its
_____ , participating in its _____ , and cooperating in
its _____—is a _____ step.

1. Church Membership Is an Opportunity to Defend the Church

   a. The Church (all believers in Christ) is _____ by its enemies.

   b. There are those who would seek to _____ from within. Being a Christ-centered,
Christ-directed member of the church is an _____ to help keep it on course.

2. Church Membership Is an Opportunity to Align with the Church's _____

   a. The local church is founded on _____ (doctrines) of the Bible.

   b. By joining with it, you help to defend its _____ .

3. Church Membership Is an Opportunity to Develop _____ Skills

   a. Churches also offer leadership training. That training not only could help you in church ministry
but also could make you more effective in _____ .

   b. Membership introduces you to the largest—and usually the most loyal—_____
_____ of the local church (Acts 2:42).

4. Church Membership Is an Opportunity to Add Strength to the Church's

_____

   a. The local church's mission is to reach unbelievers with the gospel of Jesus Christ, lead them into a
relationship with Jesus Christ, and then build them up in the faith.

   b. It also has a mandate to plant other churches. You can be a part of that exciting effort.

5. Church Membership Is an Opportunity to Have a _____ in the Church's Direction

   Your input could be one that will help the local church decide on a _____ .

6. Church Membership Is an Opportunity to Help _____

_____

   You have an opportunity to prayerfully influence the _____ and _____ of the
local church's leadership team.

7. Church Membership Is an Opportunity to _____ Your Family

   Church membership has a _____ factor.

8. Church Membership Is an Opportunity to Influence Other _____

   Finding a church and joining it is _____ to other believers.

9. Church Membership Is an Opportunity to Be a Part of the Church's

_____

You will soon discover places within the organization where you can plug in your

_____.

10. Church Membership Is an Opportunity to Help Guide the Church's _____ Decisions

a. The church organization, as well as its members, should be careful to use God's resources in a way that brings _____.

b. Your financial interest in its ministry will give you the joy of seeing the

_____.

APPENDIX G

D-I-S-C-I-P-L-E
(Developing Leaders)
Leader's Guide

9

Casting the Vision
(Leader's Guide)

Introduction

a. <u>Evangelism and discipleship</u> is just as important now as it was in the Early Church, and perhaps more.

b. Real growth is <u>conversion</u> growth. Acts 2:47, "And the Lord <u>added to their number</u> daily those who were being saved."

c. What happens to the Eurasian college student after he is saved?
   - He begins **a** <u>follow-up Bible study</u> to learn about being Christ's disciple.
   - He will have an opportunity to join a <u>small-group Bible study</u> or be part of a <u>church plant</u>.
   - Then, prayerfully, the young man's faith will be replicated in the life of another through <u>discipleship</u> training.

d. Paul's discipleship plan still works (2 Tim. 2:2): "And the things you have heard <u>me say</u> in the presence of many witnesses entrust to <u>reliable men</u> who will also be qualified to <u>teach others</u>."

e. God wants to give you 20/20 vision for <u>evangelism</u> and <u>discipleship</u>.

1. Catching the Vision

Where do I start?

(1) Start on your knees in <u>prayer</u> or in a prayer walk.

(2) Utilize a <u>plan</u>, such as big brothers/big sisters or prayer cells for enlisting believers in evangelizing or discipling.

(3) <u>Perceive it</u>. Think about what God wants to do in your community!

(4) <u>Plant it</u>. Share the vision with an accountability partner, prayer partner, or board member.

2. Casting the Vision

Draw in other <u>prayer partners</u> and share the vision with them.

3. D-I-S-C-I-P-L-E

a. Discipleship is a <u>disciplined</u> effort to become a more effective <u>follower of Jesus Christ</u>.

b. There are eight disciplines that every follower of Christ should practice:

(1) Pursuing <u>holiness</u>

(2) <u>Private</u> worship

(3) <u>Public</u> worship

(4) Observing <u>the sacraments</u>

(5) <u>Witnessing</u>

(6) <u>Discipling</u> other believers

      (7) <u>Stewardship</u>

      (8) Church <u>membership</u>

c. The best discipleship is <u>caught</u>. "Follow my example, as I follow the example of Christ" (1 Cor. 11:1).

d. Areas of concentration in developing a disciple:

      (1) **D**—<u>Develop</u> an intentional friendship.

      (2) **I**—<u>Identify</u> spiritual understanding levels.

      (3) **S**—<u>Supply</u> a support system. Your support system will include:

          (a) <u>Prayer</u>

          (b) <u>Bible study</u>

          (c) <u>Fellowship times</u>

          (d) <u>Communications</u> of encouragement

          (e) <u>Guidance</u> toward ministry

      (4) **C**—<u>Contact</u> regarding spiritual progress/needs. There is a <u>golden hour</u> of communication when you can zero-in on the needs of your disciple. In a minimum of <u>60 minutes</u> per week, you can express God's love and affirmation.

      (5) **I**—<u>Incorporate</u> into the life/ministries of the church.

      (6) **P**—<u>Pray</u> daily for spiritual growth.

      (7) **L**—<u>Look</u> for spiritual gifts. You will also need to teach them about the <u>Holy Spirit's</u> activity in giving <u>spiritual gifts</u>; and of His intent to empower those gifts through <u>entire sanctification</u>.

      (8) **E**—<u>Enlist</u> in ministry.

Oswald Chambers said, "To be a disciple means that we deliberately identify ourselves with God's interests in other people."[14]

10

Develop Intentional Relationships
(Leader's Guide)

Introduction

 a. Intentional relationships are focused attitudes and actions toward others that <u>strengthen interaction</u> and ultimately lead to a greater <u>common knowledge</u> of the Lord Jesus Christ.

 b. Perhaps one of the greatest intentional relationships of the New Testament is modeled in Christ's meeting with <u>Zacchaeus</u> (Luke 19:1-10).

 c. This incident gives us important insight into discipling others:

1. Look for the <u>Intentional Moment</u>

Jesus "was passing through." Discipling events often happen during the <u>daily routine</u>.

2. Identify the Prospect

"When Jesus reached the spot, he looked up and said to him, 'Zacchaeus . . .'" (Luke 19:5).

 a. Prospects for intentional relationships in discipleship may include:

  (1) Prebelievers who express an <u>interest</u> in church affiliation

  (2) Prebelievers who have a <u>history</u> of church affiliation

  (3) <u>New believers</u> who are just starting their faith journey

  (4) <u>Believers</u> who are struggling with personal or family faith issues

  (5) New <u>church attendees</u> who are in need of friendship

  (6) People who have been on a <u>prayer list</u>

  (7) Small-group attendees who express <u>spiritual needs</u>

 b. Intentional relationships are <u>strengthened</u> one step at a time.

 c. Your first meeting with a prebeliever or disciple should be more about <u>getting acquainted</u> than making a <u>presentation</u>.

 d. Get to know:

  (1) <u>Family</u> members

  (2) Family <u>background</u>

  (3) Church <u>background</u>

  (4) <u>Vocation</u>

  (5) <u>Hobbies</u>

  (6) <u>Favorites</u> (music, books, food, Web sites, etc.)

3. Take Intentional Risks

"'Zacchaeus, come down immediately. I must stay at your house today.' So he came down at once and welcomed him gladly. All the people saw this and began to mutter, 'He has gone to be the guest of a "sinner"'" (Luke 19:5-7).

 a. Jesus risked <u>time</u>. (An intentional relationship includes willingness to spend the time necessary to let that person know you are sincerely interested in him or her.)

 b. Jesus risked <u>reputation</u>. "He has gone to be the guest of a 'sinner.'" Establishing an intentional relationship with another may include going to that person's "turf."

  (1) Making a brief appearance at a function

  (2) Greeting the person who invited you

133

(3) And then politely making your exit

c. Jesus risked <u>acceptance</u>. "Zacchaeus stood up and said to the Lord, 'Look, Lord! Here and now I give half of my possessions to the poor, and if I have cheated anybody out of anything, I will pay back four times the amount'" (Luke 19:8).

d. Jesus risked <u>forgiveness</u>. "Jesus said to him, 'Today salvation has come to this house'" (v. 9*a*).

e. Jesus risked <u>association</u>. "This man, too, is a son of Abraham. For the Son of Man came to seek and to save what was lost" (vv. 9*b*-10).

    (1) Prebelievers are often afraid to lose the <u>emotional support</u> of family and friends.

    (2) You will need to <u>develop your friendship</u> with them.

4. Minister like Jesus

a. Jesus met people at their <u>point of need</u> (Mark 10:51-52).

b. Jesus helped people believe they could become <u>better than they were</u> (Matt. 4:19).

c. Jesus pointed <u>a way out</u> of hopeless situations (John 11:21-26).

d. Jesus <u>never gave up</u> on people (Luke 22:32).

e. Jesus gave with no <u>thought of return</u> (Matt. 16:25).

f. Jesus always encouraged people to <u>make the extra effort</u> (Matt. 5:41).

g. Jesus relied on the <u>Scriptures</u> (Matt. 4:4).

h. Jesus was always <u>on a mission</u> (Luke 2:49).

i. Jesus never compromised His <u>character</u> (Matt. 4:9-10).

j. Jesus taught with <u>compassion</u> (Matt. 9:35-36).

k. Jesus lived a life of <u>joy</u> (Luke 10:21).

l. Jesus prayed <u>continually</u> (Luke 6:12).

m. Jesus observed people <u>carefully</u> (Mark 12:41).

n. Jesus lived <u>simply</u> (Matt. 8:20).

o. Jesus forgave without <u>expectations</u> (Matt. 18:21-22).

p. Jesus obeyed the Father <u>no matter the cost</u> (Matt. 26:42).

11

Identify Spiritual Understanding Levels
(Leader's Guide)

Introduction

Philip the disciple was on a missionary trip when he met a member of Queen Candace's royal court, who was reading the Scriptures. It turned into a discipling ministry: Acts 8:26-40.

(1) He <u>obeyed</u> the Spirit's leading (vv. 26-27). God will make the <u>appointment</u>; you will need to be open to His Spirit's leading.

(2) He <u>identified</u> a spiritual understanding level (vv. 30-31). To <u>provide the spiritual help</u> needed, he had to discover the official's level of spiritual understanding.

(3) He <u>taught him</u> from his level of understanding (vv. 34-35). He discovered an <u>entry level</u> and began to teach accordingly.

(4) He <u>encouraged him</u> to the next level (vv. 36-38). Help the disciple understand the importance of religious practices in light of being <u>born again</u> or of being <u>sanctified</u>.

(5) He <u>released</u> him (vv. 39-40). Discipleship has both <u>short-range</u> and <u>long-range</u> dimensions. At the appropriate time, new disciples are trusted to make some <u>discoveries</u> on their own—yet remaining on the prayer list and contact list of the discipler.

Levels of Understanding

a. Philip's discipleship encounter teaches about the importance of discerning the <u>spiritual needs</u> of others.

b. As a discipler you will need to know <u>where to begin</u>.

c. There are at least <u>three levels</u> of spiritual understanding and a proposed teaching path.

  (1) *Level one: the prebeliever*

    Christ himself taught us about reaching out to people in the scriptural account of the meeting with the Samaritan woman at the well (John 4:4-30).

    (a) He established an <u>intentional</u> friendship (vv. 7-9).
- He met the Samaritan at her point of need, no matter the <u>opinion of others</u>.
- Intentional friendship has an end goal of <u>presenting the gospel</u>. Some conversation starters may include:
  - Religious <u>affiliation</u>
  - <u>Social issues</u> and their relationship to faith
  - <u>Opinions</u> about God
  - <u>World situations</u>
- Responses will give insights
  - Knowledge of the <u>Bible</u>
  - A "<u>worldview</u>" (atheistic, agnostic, pluralistic, etc.)
  - Personal or spiritual <u>issues</u>

    (b) He developed an <u>interest</u> (vv. 10-11). It was merely a link to the more important subject: the condition of <u>the woman's soul</u>.

    (c) He made a thought-provoking <u>statement</u> (vv. 16-18). Jesus brought the woman to a point of <u>admitting her need</u>.

    (d) He gave her a glimpse of <u>hope</u> (vv. 23-24). Jesus showed her <u>a better way</u>.

    (e) He taught her about <u>the truth</u> of God's Word (v. 26). One-on-one discipleship is leading a person to an encounter with the <u>claims of the Word of God</u>.

  (2) *Level two: new believer*

- One who has recently made a decision to <u>follow Christ</u>.
- The disciple Ananias's spiritual mentoring of Saul (later named Paul) is a gold standard (Acts 9:10-20).

(a) He <u>took the risk</u> (vv. 11-13). Ananias had heard about Saul's former lifestyle. But he was compelled by the Holy Spirit to take on the assignment—no matter the personal cost. Discipleship is often costly.

(b) He <u>approached him</u> (v. 17*ab*).
  - Ananias let Saul know they were on <u>common ground</u>. Saul's whole world had been turned upside down.
  - Your task as a discipler is to let them know that you are concerned about their <u>transition</u>.

(c) He <u>taught him</u> (vv. 17*c*-18). Ananias began to explain "the Way" to Saul.
  - He familiarized him with the <u>basics</u> of the Christian faith.
  - He advised him on Christian <u>ethics</u> and a Christian <u>lifestyle</u>.
  - He encouraged him to use his <u>education</u>, <u>knowledge</u>, and <u>skills</u> in ministry.

(d) He <u>released him</u> (vv. 19-20).
  - Ananias wasn't <u>threatened</u> by Paul's abilities.
  - Ananias recognized they were God-given, and served God's <u>master plan</u> for the church.

(3) *Uncommitted or unassigned believer*

(a) You may be asked to encourage more established believers to make a next-level <u>commitment</u>.
  - Small <u>groups</u>
  - Church <u>administration</u>
  - Volunteer <u>ministries</u>
  - Mission <u>trips</u>

(b) You may also be asked to encourage a fellow believer to make a stronger commitment to the local church through <u>church membership</u>.

(c) Aquila and Priscilla were members of the Early Church who made *next-level* commitments (Acts 18:1-26). Paul (formerly Saul) saw they had <u>great potential</u> to be ministers and disciplers and encouraged them toward ministry.
  - He <u>befriended</u> them (vv. 2-3).
  - He <u>mentored</u> them (v. 4).
  - He <u>launched</u> them (v. 19).

(d) Your task is not only to teach the new disciples the "principles of flight" but also to encourage them to "<u>fly</u>."

12

Supply a Support System
(Leader's Guide)

Introduction

   a. Encouraging the disciple to a next-level commitment takes a <u>focused and purposeful effort</u>.

   b. The basic qualities of <u>commitment</u>, <u>concern</u>, <u>communication</u>, and <u>concentrated training</u> must be present in each discipleship assignment.

   c. Those qualities should be present in a <u>support system</u> for your disciple, no matter his or her level of spiritual understanding.

1. New Believer

The apostle Paul called the disciple Timothy his "<u>son</u>" in the faith. Discipling a new believer might be compared to a parent's care for a <u>newborn child</u>.

- <u>Four areas of development</u>: motor skills, hearing, vision, and communication.[15]
- Those principles are seen in the apostle Paul's <u>prayers</u> for his disciples:

   a. <u>Motor skills</u>: **building movement and coordination** (Col. 1:9-12).

   (1) He prayed for their growth in <u>knowledge</u> (v. 9). He prayed that the Holy Spirit would <u>impress biblical truth</u> on their minds. Supply your disciple with a support system of <u>Bible study</u>. Guidelines:
   - Don't be afraid of <u>questions</u>.
   - Don't be <u>sidetracked</u> by personal issues.
   - Don't assume that your student knows how to <u>get around in the Bible</u>.
   - Don't tackle the "<u>big ones</u>."
   - Don't <u>give up</u> (Isa. 55:11).

   (2) He prayed for their growth in <u>character</u> (Col. 1:10).
   - Paul was concerned that Christians be <u>steady in their walk</u>.
   - Paul prayed that his disciples would <u>learn to be leaders</u>.

   (3) He prayed for their <u>strong finish</u> (vv. 11-12).
   - Be <u>positive</u>.
   - Point out the <u>hope</u>.
   - Remind them of the <u>finish</u>: heaven.

   b. <u>Hearing</u>: **Responding to voices and other sounds** (2 Cor. 13:7-9).
   Paul wanted his disciples to trust in <u>God's power</u>, not human effort.
   - Provide your disciple with a support system of <u>spiritual discernment</u>.
     - God never speaks contrary to <u>His Word</u>.
     - God never leads contrary to <u>conscience</u>.
     - God uses the <u>counsel of other Christians</u>.
     - God can even use <u>adversity</u> to strengthen the disciple.

   (1) Your availability when your disciple is facing tempting times will be a great source of <u>encouragement and strength</u>.

   (2) Let your disciple know <u>how human you are</u>.

   (3) Encourage your disciple to a life of <u>holiness</u>.
   - Provide literature and a study that will teach about <u>entire sanctification</u>.
   - Share your testimony of how you discovered the power of <u>Spirit-filled living</u>.

   c. <u>Vision</u>: **Learning to focus** (Eph. 1:18-21).
   - Paul was a <u>purpose-driven</u> man (Phil. 3:13-14).

137

- He encouraged those whom he led to focus their attention on the future <u>rather than the past.</u>
  - (1) He prayed that they would be people of a <u>clean heart</u> (Eph. 1:18*a*). Help your disciple learn how to <u>focus on Christ</u>.
  - (2) He prayed that they would know about <u>true riches</u> (v. 18*b*). Make a difference in your disciple's worldview:
    - Teach about God's <u>ownership</u>.
    - Teach about <u>giving back</u> to God.
    - Teach about the principle of <u>the tithe</u>.
    - Teach about the hope of <u>eternal life</u>.
    - Teach about investments of <u>time, talent, treasure</u>.
  - (3) He prayed that they would understand <u>Christ's rule</u> (vv. 19*b*-21*a*). Teach your disciple about end time hope.

  d. **<u>Communication</u>: expressing affection** (Phil. 1:9-11).
  - Paul was concerned that disciples understood the depths of commitment and interdependence that come with being a part of <u>God's family</u>.
  - Christianity includes the <u>emotions</u> as well as the will. Guide the disciple in making wise decisions regarding <u>relationships</u>.

2. Newly Committed Believer

The discipler is also a <u>coach</u>: provides training and guidance for committed believers who have taken next-level steps of growth or ministry.

  a. Try to determine the disciple's level of <u>spiritual understanding</u>.

  b. Evaluate the disciple's <u>personal experience</u>.

  c. Observe <u>personal characteristics</u>.

  d. Evaluate the disciple's <u>readiness</u>.

You will multiply your own ministry many times over through the dedicated service of one in whom you have invested your life.

13

Contact Regarding Spiritual Progress/Needs
(Leader's Guide)

Introduction

In emergency care there is a window of time known as the golden hour, where patients under treatment have the greatest likelihood of <u>survival</u>.

1. Golden Hour Contacts

    a. There is a <u>window of opportunity</u>, a golden hour, when focused care is crucial to the spiritual survival of the disciple or when the desired spiritual effect is best achieved.

    b. The golden hour is an accumulated <u>60 minutes</u> of focused contact time each week.

    c. Several <u>means of communication</u> may be included in the golden hour contact time:
- <u>Telephone call</u>
- <u>E-mail, text message</u> (and instant message)
- <u>Note or card</u>
- <u>Personal appointment</u>
- <u>Relational event</u>

2. Contact Protocol

    a. Build a quality <u>relationship</u>.

    b. Anything that is said to be "<u>off the record</u>" should be exactly that.

    c. Keep the relationship <u>on the level</u>.

    d. Make sure the contacts have <u>time parameters</u>.

    e. Use the type of contact that <u>fits the disciple</u>.

    f. Make sure the contact has an <u>end goal</u> of spiritual growth.

3. Contact Methods

    a. Telephone call

        (1) Make sure a telephone call is <u>welcomed</u>.

        (2) Make brevity your <u>goal</u>.

            (a) Express your <u>concern</u>.

            (b) Check on <u>progress or needs</u>.

            (c) Strengthen an <u>intentional</u> relationship.

        (3) Prayerfully think about <u>what you will say</u>.

        (4) Make it a <u>friendly</u> call.

        (5) Make it a <u>purposeful</u> call.

            (a) Listen for the <u>tone of voice</u>.

            (b) Respond according to the <u>tone of the conversation</u>.

            (c) List <u>prayer requests</u>.

            (d) Pick out and quote an <u>encouraging Bible verse</u>.

            (e) Discuss a book, chapter, or verse from the Bible that <u>has impacted your disciple</u>.

            (f) Remind your disciple that you are continually <u>praying for him or her</u>.

b. E-mail or text messaging

    (1) E-mail

        (a) Use <u>personal</u> rather than business address.

        (b) Don't "<u>copy</u>" message to others.

        (c) Prayerfully think about the <u>content</u>.

        (d) Make the message <u>brief</u>.

        (e) Be <u>consistent</u>.

        (f) Be <u>positive</u>.

        (g) Limit the e-mails to <u>one or two</u> each week.

        (h) Avoid including or attaching "<u>pass-along</u>" content.

        (i) Include a <u>Bible verse</u>.

        (j) Check for <u>grammar and spelling</u>.

        (k) Remind your disciple of your <u>prayers</u>.

        (l) Remind your disciple of your <u>availability</u>.

    (2) Text messages

        (a) Avoid "<u>cutesy</u>" content.

        (b) Get right to the <u>point</u>.

        (c) Remind your disciple of your <u>prayers</u>.

        (d) Include a Scripture <u>reference</u> rather than an entire verse (e.g., John 3:16).

        (e) Be <u>consistent</u>.

        (f) Limit the <u>number</u> of messages.

    (3) Instant messages (IM) or video conferencing

c. Note or card

    (1) Use notes or cards for encouraging or recognizing a <u>milestone</u>.

    (2) <u>Teaching</u> and strengthening.

    (3) Time of <u>crisis</u>.

    (4) Reinforce <u>service</u>.

    (5) Give <u>assurance</u>.

    (6) <u>Spiritual</u> milestone.

    (7) Recognize an <u>award</u>.

d. Personal appointment

    (1) Some of Jesus' most memorable discipling was <u>one-on-one</u>:

        (a) Nicodemus

        (b) Zacchaeus

        (c) Peter

        (d) Mary and Martha

    (2) Guidelines:

        (a) Set a time that will be <u>unhurried</u>.

        (b) Determine to meet within <u>time</u> parameters.

        (c) Avoid disrupting family or work <u>schedules</u>.

        (d) Avoid conflicting with church <u>events</u>.

        (e) Send a <u>reminder</u>.

        (f) Pick up the <u>tab</u> (restaurant meetings).

        (g) Make a <u>follow-up</u> contact.

    (3) Include:

        (a) <u>Encouragement</u>

        (b) Praise for <u>efforts</u>

        (c) <u>Progress</u> or needs

        (d) <u>Q & A</u>

(e) Inquiry into personal or family <u>needs</u>

(f) Church <u>event</u> reminders

(g) Brief <u>prayer</u>

(h) Bible <u>verse(s)</u>

4. Making the Golden Hour Golden

a. <u>Scaling back</u> or changing directions

<u>Signs</u> that the discipling effort can be scaled back or change directions:

(1) The disciple is making obvious <u>spiritual progress</u>.

(2) The relationship has a different <u>dynamic</u>.

(3) The disciple has reached a "<u>discipler</u>" level.

b. <u>Maximizing</u> discipling effectiveness

(1) Keep your <u>purpose</u> in mind.

(2) Stay <u>alert</u>.

(3) Know your <u>limits</u>.

14

Incorporate into the Life and Ministries of the Church
(Leader's Guide)

Introduction

    a. New disciples need the <u>life and ministries</u> of a local church (Heb. 10:25).

        (1) Some have <u>never</u> attended church.

            (a) Speak <u>positively</u> of your own church background.

            (b) Include a study of the <u>church</u> in your discipling.

            (c) Invite them to be your guests for a <u>worship service</u>, followed by a fellowship time.

            (d) Encourage them to take a <u>baptism</u> or <u>new Christian</u> class.

            (e) Reinforce the importance of making a <u>public declaration</u> of their new faith commitment.

            (f) Reinforce the importance of worshipping with <u>fellow believers</u>, including the reading and study of <u>the Bible</u> in a structured environment.

        (2) Some have <u>been turned off</u> by the church.

            (a) <u>Listen fairly</u> to their opinions and attitudes of the church.

            (b) <u>Speak positively</u> of your own church background.

            (c) Introduce them to <u>age-related</u>, positive role models in the church.

        (3) Some have <u>abandoned</u> the church.

            (a) Listen sympathetically to <u>their story</u>.

            (b) <u>Speak positively</u> of your own church background.

            (c) Reinforce the <u>importance of worshipping</u> with other believers, including the reading and study of the Bible in a structured environment.

            (d) <u>Invite them</u> to a worship service as your guests, followed by a fellowship time.

            (e) Reinforce the necessity of <u>ministry</u> as an outworking of their faith.

    b. Incorporating the new disciple into the life and ministries of the church can be done at several important "<u>entry points</u>."

1. Baptism and the Lord's Supper

    a. <u>Baptism</u>

    Action Plan: <u>Sponsor</u> the disciple's scheduled baptism (plan a fellowship time, including providing refreshments, following the baptismal service and child care during and after the ceremony).

    b. <u>The Lord's Supper</u>

    Action Plan

    (1) Discuss the <u>meaning</u> of the Lord's Supper observance.

    (2) Sit with the disciple and <u>share in the observance</u>.

2. Worship Event

Action Plan

    a. Discuss the need for <u>public</u> and private worship.

    b. Invite them (along with their friends and family) to <u>sit with you during worship</u>.

    c. Introduce them to other <u>attendees</u> (especially age-/interest-related attendees).

    d. Make sure they have a <u>worship folder</u> and church <u>brochure</u>.

    e. Invite them to <u>dinner or refreshments</u> following the service.

3. Special Event

    a. Events

        (1) Christmas and Easter <u>pageants</u>

        (2) <u>Dinners</u>

        (3) Church <u>daycare</u> celebrations

        (4) <u>Auctions</u>

        (5) Church <u>anniversaries</u>

        (6) <u>Revivals</u>

        (7) Missions <u>conventions</u>

        (8) <u>Concerts</u>

    b. Action Plan

        (1) Invite and <u>remind</u> the disciple of the event.

        (2) Explain the <u>purpose</u> of the event, including sending advertising.

        (3) Assist with <u>reservations or tickets</u>.

        (4) Give <u>map directions</u>.

        (5) Plan a follow-up meeting or fellowship time <u>within two weeks of the event</u>, inviting other attendees, members, and church staff.

        (6) Encourage <u>volunteerism</u> for the next event.

4. Small Group

    a. Groups

        (1) <u>Sunday School class</u>

        (2) <u>Bible study</u>

        (3) <u>Prayer cell</u>

    b. Action Plan

        (1) <u>Invite and remind</u> the disciple about the group meeting.

        (2) Explain the <u>purpose</u> of the small group.

        (3) Provide <u>study guides or other materials</u>.

        (4) Deflect questions to the disciple that would make the disciple uncomfortable by <u>turning the questions to you</u> or answering them in a <u>generalized</u> way.

        (5) Give the disciple an opportunity to <u>host</u> a small group.

        (6) Encourage <u>volunteerism</u> in set-up or teaching (when appropriate).

        (7) Schedule a <u>fellowship time</u> that will include the disciple and other group members.

5. Interest Group

    Action Plan

    a. Provide <u>information</u> about the interest group, including map directions, times, locations.

    b. <u>Introduce</u> the disciple to other group members.

    c. <u>Attend</u> group special events that include your disciple (musicals, drama, sporting events).

    c. <u>Remind</u> disciples of your prayers regarding their participation.

6. Ministry Team

    Action Plan

    a. Pray for your disciple's ministry <u>awareness</u>.

    b. Provide information on ministry <u>teams</u>.

c. Alert ministry team <u>leaders</u> of your disciple's interests and abilities.

d. <u>Guide</u> your disciple toward a team.

e. Offer to be a <u>prayer partner</u>.

f. Help provide <u>sponsorship</u> for team events.

15

Pray Daily for Spiritual Growth
(Leader's Guide)

Introduction

 a. Disciples need a <u>support</u> team.

 b. Prayer is a <u>weapon</u> of warfare (Eph. 6:12).

 c. Christian living is a <u>team</u> effort (1 Cor. 12:12).

 d. Prayer is a form of spiritual <u>strength training</u>.

1. Interdependence

 a. Pray for your disciple's <u>faithfulness in worship</u>.

 b. Pray for your disciple's <u>obedience</u> to the Holy Spirit's guidance.

 c. Pray for your disciple's <u>Bible study</u> times.

 d. Pray that your disciple will pursue <u>holiness</u>.

 e. Pray that your disciple will <u>influence</u> others for Christ.

2. Prayer Partnerships

 a. Two or more believers may <u>team up</u> to pray for prebelievers, new believers, or other believers.

 b. Biblical history proves there is <u>power in partnerships</u>:

  (1) Two <u>brothers</u> were called to be disciples (Matt. 4:18, 21).

  (2) Two <u>disciples</u> were sent to prepare for Jesus' entrance into Jerusalem (Matt. 21:1-3).

  (3) Disciples were sent out to minister <u>two by two</u> (Mark 6:7).

  (4) Seventy disciples were sent out to minister <u>two by two</u> (Luke 10:1).

"Again I say to you that if two of you agree on earth concerning anything that they ask, it will be done for them by My Father in heaven" (Matt. 18:19, NKJV).

 c. Prayer partners

  (1) Strengthen individual <u>courage</u>

  (2) Help to offset individual <u>weaknesses</u>

  (3) Keep each other <u>focused</u>

  (4) Remind each other of prayer <u>concerns</u>

  (5) Widen the area of <u>influence</u>

 d. Prayer partnerships are <u>practical</u>.

 e. Prayer partnerships may be used <u>in addition</u> to individual prayer.

  (1) **What is a prayer partnership?**

   (a) An <u>agreement</u> between two or more people to pray daily

   (b) For <u>people</u> on their <u>prayer list</u>

   (c) For a specified <u>period of time</u>

   (d) In agreement with <u>Matt. 18:19</u>

  (2) **What do prayer partners do?**

  Prayer partners <u>pray together</u> either in person, by phone, or by other appropriate means (e.g., video conferencing).

  (3) **How should prayer partnerships be formed?**

   (a) Prayer partnerships may be formed from an <u>organized</u> prayer effort, such as prayer cells or big brothers/big sisters discipling ministries.

(b) Prayer partnerships may be formed from <u>friendships</u> or <u>staff relationships</u> within the church.

(4) **What are the qualifications of a prayer partner?**
  (a) Complete a <u>basic Bible study</u> or discipleship course
  (b) Complete a prayer partner <u>training session</u>
  (c) Active in the <u>church</u> (preferably members)
  (d) Disciples who have a <u>solid witness</u>
  (e) Able to keep <u>confidences</u>
  (f) Known for <u>faithfulness</u>
  (g) Of the same <u>age range</u>

(5) **When and where should prayer partners meet?**

  Prayer partners should plan to meet at least <u>once</u> each week.

(6) **What should be included in prayer partner meetings?**
  (a) Sharing <u>Bible promises</u> regarding prayer or faith
  (b) Sharing of prayer concerns from the <u>prayer list</u>
  (c) Mutual <u>encouragement</u>
  (d) <u>Praying</u> for the other prayer partner
  (e) <u>Praising God</u> for answered prayer

(7) **Who should the prayer partners pray for?**
  (a) Primarily the <u>needs</u> of a prebeliever, new believer, or other believers.
  (b) Other <u>names</u> may be provided by the prayer coordinator, a pastoral staff member, or from big brothers/big sisters or prayer cells.

(8) **How long should a prayer partnership last?**
  (a) Some will <u>remain prayer partners</u> for a long period of time.
  (b) Some will form a prayer partnership for an <u>immediate or short-term need</u>.
  (c) The length of time depends on such factors as:
    • The <u>compatibility</u> of the prayer partners
    • The <u>urgency</u> of the need
    • The <u>support</u> of staff, friends, or family
    • The <u>answer</u> to a prayer concern

(9) **How can prayer partnerships be multiplied?**
  • As <u>answers to prayer are announced</u> to the prayer partners and to the congregation (including answered prayer from your own discipling effort), enthusiasm will begin to build for prayer partnerships.
  • <u>Testimonies</u> of new faith commitments may be part of a public worship service.
  (a) <u>Announce</u> that new prayer partnerships will soon be formed.
    • Launch a three- to four-week <u>message series</u> or short-term <u>class</u> on prayer.
    • Include <u>Bible verses</u> on prayer and faith in print publications or electronic announcements.
    • Announce <u>answers</u> to prayer in worship services or small-group meetings.
    • Include <u>video clips</u> on prayer in worship services.
    • Place <u>signage</u> that includes Bible verses or quotes about prayer in high-traffic areas of the church or meeting place.
    • Have one or more <u>prayer partners</u> write a 50- to 100-word <u>article</u> on what prayer partnerships have meant to them (letting them know in advance that the article may be edited for word count and content).
  (b) Organize a <u>one-session</u> prayer partnerships <u>training</u> class.
  (c) <u>Conduct</u> the prayer partnerships class (120 minutes).
    • Session 1: How to Pray for Others (intercessory prayer) (30 minutes)
    • Break (10 minutes)

- Session 2: The Duties of a Prayer Partner (amplified lesson from the "Duties of a Prayer Partner" handout) (30 minutes)
- Form prayer partnerships (20 minutes)
  - Ask for <u>volunteer</u> partnerships.
  - <u>Appoint</u> partnerships.
  - Have the prayer partners <u>meet</u> for brief prayer time.

(d) <u>Introduce</u> prayer partners in a worship service or meeting. Have congregation members <u>submit</u> prayer requests on prayer request cards.

(e) <u>Compile and assign</u> prayer requests in a post-service event meeting.
  - Compile <u>duplicate</u> lists on prayer list cards.
  - Place the <u>prayer list cards</u> in church stationery envelopes.
  - Distribute <u>envelopes</u> to prayer partnerships.
  - <u>Give</u> encouragement and instruction.
  - Close in <u>prayer</u>.

Remember the words of Jesus to His disciple: "I have prayed for you . . . that your faith may not fail" (Luke 22:32).

16

Look for Spiritual Gifts
(Leader's Guide)

Introduction

    a. <u>Abilities</u> and <u>personalities</u> are part of God's master design (Eph. 4:11-16).

    b. Abilities and personalities surrendered fully to Jesus Christ are <u>channels</u> through which He reaches the lost and strengthens His church (Acts 1:8).

1. What Are the Differences Between the *Fruit* of the Spirit and the *Gifts* of the Spirit?

Fruit	Gifts
1. Defines what a Christian <u>is</u>	1. Determines what a Christian <u>does</u>
2. <u>Same</u> in every Christian	2. <u>Different</u> in each Christian
3. <u>Singular</u>	3. <u>Plural</u>
4. Satan <u>cannot</u> imitate	4. Satan <u>can</u> imitate
5. Deals with <u>character</u>	5. Deals with <u>service ministry</u>
6. <u>End</u> in itself	6. <u>Means</u> to an end
7. <u>Permanent/eternal</u>	7. <u>Will cease</u>
8. According to <u>spirituality and maturity</u>	8. <u>Not according</u> to spirituality

2. What Is a Spiritual Gift?

    a. Spiritual gifts are divinely enabled <u>abilities</u>.

    b. Spiritual gifts are used in helping to fulfill Christ's <u>mission</u>.

    c. Believers should seek to discover what Spirit-enabled abilities they may possess. How?

        (1) Identify <u>interests</u> that support Christ's mission.

        (2) Identify natural <u>talent</u> that would fulfill that interest.

        (3) <u>Reflect</u> on how those interests and talents may be used for Christ.

        (4) Look for <u>opportunities</u> to utilize interests and talents in mission supporting efforts.

    d. The greatest gift is the <u>Spirit himself</u> (Acts 2:15-17).

3. To Whom Are Spiritual Gifts Given?

    a. Spiritual gifts are given to <u>followers of Jesus Christ</u> (1 Cor. 12:7).

    b. Spiritual gifts are "activated" or "released" when a person is <u>spiritually reborn</u> (1 Cor. 12:13).

    c. The Holy Spirit, the giver of spiritual gifts, <u>indwells</u> the new believer (Acts 2:38).

    d. Believers do not "<u>choose</u>" their gifts. They are given to them by Christ in accordance with His will (1 Cor. 12:11).

    e. No one believer has all of <u>the spiritual gifts</u>, nor is any one gift common to all.

4. What Is the Purpose of Spiritual Gifts?

Spiritual gifts help fulfill the broader, eternal scope of God's promises.

    a. They <u>qualify</u>: "To prepare God's people for works of service" (Eph. 4:12*a*). They also are "<u>tools</u>" used to

        (1) <u>Communicate</u> the good news of the gospel to prebelievers

        (2) <u>Encourage</u> and enlighten believers by the Word of God

        (3) <u>Organize</u> the church into a functioning body

(4) <u>Enlist</u> the church in accomplishing growth

b. They <u>edify</u>: "So that the body of Christ may be built up" (v. 12*b*).

c. They <u>unify</u>: "Until we all reach unity in the faith and in the knowledge of the Son of God" (v. 13*a*).

d. They <u>fortify</u>: "Become mature, attaining to the whole measure of the fullness of Christ" (v. 13*b*).

e. They <u>exemplify</u>: "Then we will no longer be infants, tossed back and forth by the waves, and blown here and there by every wind of teaching and by the cunning and craftiness of men in their deceitful scheming. Instead, speaking the truth in love, we will in all things grow up into him who is the Head, that is, Christ" (vv. 14-15).

f. They <u>glorify</u>: "From him the whole body, joined and held together by every supporting ligament, grows and builds itself up in love, as each part does its work" (v. 16).

5. How Do *Human Talents* and Spiritual *Gifts* Differ?

a. Abilities are the <u>raw materials</u> that God blesses and empowers to accomplish His eternal purpose.

b. Distributed and anointed by the Holy Spirit, they are <u>made alive</u> through their dedication to Christ and His cause.

(1) One spiritual gift is not <u>more important</u> than another.

(2) They are not to be used as personal <u>attention-getters</u>.

(3) They are to be used to bring attention to <u>Christ</u>.

(4) They should not be at the source of <u>division</u> between believers; they should be a source of <u>unity</u>.

Talents	Gifts
1. <u>Inherited</u> from forefathers	1. Given by the <u>Holy Spirit</u>
2. Present from <u>natural birth</u>	2. Present from <u>new birth</u>
3. God-given to <u>all</u> members of the human race	3. God-given to members of <u>Christ's body</u>
4. For <u>human</u> activities	4. For ministry of the <u>Body</u>
5. Can be operated <u>independently</u> of the Holy Spirit	5. <u>Dependent</u> on the Holy Spirit
6. Ministers primarily on a <u>natural</u> level	6. Ministers on a <u>spiritual</u> level
7. Effects are usually <u>temporal/finite</u>	7. Effects are <u>eternal/infinite</u>
8. Glorifies <u>self</u>	8. Glorifies <u>God</u>

6. Discovering Spiritual Gifts

Helping disciples discover abilities that may be used in Kingdom-building is essential to their <u>spiritual growth</u> and the <u>growth of the church</u>.

a. Introduce them to a spiritual gifts <u>survey</u>.

b. <u>Point out</u> the abilities that could be used in the church.

c. Make their discovery of their spiritual gifts a matter of <u>mutual prayer</u>.

d. Help them see how a <u>Spirit-filled life</u> will bring wholeness—and holiness—to their spiritual journey.

149

17

Enlist in Ministry
(Leader's Guide)

Introduction

a. Nowhere does the "light" of a disciple's life bring a warmer and brighter glow than through the <u>ministries</u> of the church (1 Cor. 12:27-31).

b. You are the <u>coach-encourager</u> who will teach your disciples how to take an active part in church ministry.
   (1) Through <u>training</u>
   (2) Through <u>internship</u> with another
   (3) Through <u>appointment</u> to a specific position
   (4) Through <u>discipling</u> another
   (5) Through <u>prayer</u> ministries
   (6) Through <u>small groups</u>

Not only will you encourage them to find a place of ministry, but you will also guide them in enlisting in that ministry—always in cooperation with the leadership of the church.

1. Local Church Ministry

a. The church is "organizational machinery" that needs both <u>parts and labor</u>.

b. The "parts" make the machinery <u>run</u>, while the "labor" keeps it <u>running</u>! And the Holy Spirit's presence and power keeps it <u>fueled and lubricated</u>.

c. There is a place for your disciple's interest and ability.
   (1) List the <u>types</u> of ministries.
   (2) Consult with local church leadership about needed <u>volunteers</u>.
   (3) Ask local church leadership to supply <u>job descriptions</u> for volunteer needs.
   (4) <u>Evaluate</u> your disciple's ability and experience.
   (5) Match <u>abilities and experience</u> with volunteer needs.
   (6) <u>Approach</u> your disciple with volunteer possibilities.
   (7) Recommend a volunteer <u>position</u>.

2. Missions Ministry

a. The church also has a <u>global mission</u> (Luke 10:1-2).

b. Spiritual mentoring can encourage your disciple to have a "<u>global vision</u>."
   (1) Teach them about Christ's global <u>commission</u>.
   (2) Share missions <u>publications</u> with them.
   (3) Invite them to assist with a missions <u>convention</u>.
   (4) Tell them how your <u>missions</u> involvement has benefited you.
   (5) Encourage them to participate in a missions <u>trip</u>.
   (6) Encourage <u>correspondence</u> for or with overseas missionaries.
   (7) Encourage them to be <u>prayer partners</u> with an overseas missionary.
   (8) Encourage them to <u>support</u> a mission or missionary.
   (9) Inform them of <u>denominational</u> missions opportunities.
   (10) Teach them about <u>next-level</u> missions ministry (short-term or vocational missions opportunity).

3. Compassionate Ministry

a. Your disciples must understand that their own <u>community</u> is a mission field.

b. Enlisting them in <u>compassionate ministries</u> is a great place to start.

c. Compassionate ministries minister to the whole person—<u>spiritually</u>, <u>physically</u>, <u>emotionally</u>, <u>socially</u>, and <u>financially</u>.

d. Disciples' experiences with compassionate ministries may be just the beginning of a <u>wider</u> ministry—including <u>vocational</u> ministry.

    (1) Study compassionate ministries in the <u>Scriptures</u>.

    (2) Acquaint them with ministry <u>opportunities</u> in the community.

    (3) Ask them to <u>help you</u> with a compassionate ministry on-site.

    (4) Introduce them to community compassionate ministries <u>leaders</u>.

    (5) Inform them of <u>denominational</u> compassionate ministries.

4. Small-Group Ministry

a. Small groups, such as a neighborhood Bible studies, big brothers/big sisters or prayer cells is an exciting <u>introduction</u> to ministry.

b. Small groups are good <u>training</u> grounds.

c. Working in a small group setting usually builds <u>self-confidence</u>.

d. Training and supervision provide a <u>support system</u>.

e. Encourage volunteerism in small groups as a way of enriching <u>Bible study skills</u> and utilizing <u>spiritual gifts</u>.

5. Event Ministry

a. Special events offer both the discipler and the disciple a time of <u>training</u> and hands-on <u>experience</u>.

b. Your disciple will see <u>ministry in action</u>.

APPENDIX H

D-I-S-C-I-P-L-E
(Developing Leaders)
Student's Guide

9

Casting the Vision
(Student's Guide)

Introduction

a. _____ is just as important now as it was in the Early Church, and perhaps more.

b. Real growth is _____ growth. Acts 2:47, "And the Lord _____ _____ daily those who were being saved."

c. What happens to the Eurasian college student after he is saved?
  - He begins a _____ to learn about being Christ's disciple.
  - He will have an opportunity to join a _____ or be part of a _____.
  - Then, prayerfully, the young man's faith will be replicated in the life of another through _____ training.

d. Paul's discipleship plan still works (2 Tim. 2:2): "And the things you have heard _____ in the presence of many witnesses entrust to _____ who will also be qualified to _____."

e. God wants to give you 20/20 vision for _____ and _____.

1. Catching the Vision

Where do I start?

(1) Start on your knees in _____ or in a prayer walk.

(2) Utilize a _____, such as big brothers/big sisters or prayer cells for enlisting believers in evangelizing or discipling.

(3) _____. Think about what God wants to do in your community!

(4) _____. Share the vision with an accountability partner, prayer partner, or board member.

2. Casting the Vision

Draw in other _____ and share the vision with them.

3. D-I-S-C-I-P-L-E

a. Discipleship is a _____ effort to become a more effective _____ _____.

b. There are eight disciplines that every follower of Christ should practice:
  (1) Pursuing _____

(2) _____ worship

(3) _____ worship

(4) Observing _____

(5) _____

(6) _____ other believers

(7) _____

(8) Church _____

c. The best discipleship is _____. "Follow my example, as I follow the example of Christ" (1 Cor. 11:1).

d. Areas of concentration in developing a disciple:

(1) D—_____ an intentional friendship.

(2) I—_____ spiritual understanding levels.

(3) S—_____ a support system. Your support system will include:

   (a) _____

   (b) _____

   (c) _____

   (d) _____ of encouragement

   (e) _____ toward ministry

(4) C—_____ regarding spiritual progress/needs. There is a _____ _____ of communication when you can zero-in on the needs of your disciple. In a minimum of _____ per week, you can express God's love and affirmation.

(5) I—_____ into the life/ministries of the church.

(6) P—_____ daily for spiritual growth.

(7) L—_____ for spiritual gifts. You will also need to teach them about the _____ _____ activity in giving _____; and of His intent to empower those gifts through _____.

(8) E—_____ in ministry.

Oswald Chambers said, "To be a disciple means that we deliberately identify ourselves with God's interests in other people."[16]

10

Develop Intentional Relationships
(Student's Guide)

Introduction

    a. Intentional relationships are focused attitudes and actions toward others that _____ _____ and ultimately lead to a greater _____ _____ of the Lord Jesus Christ.

    b. Perhaps one of the greatest intentional relationships of the New Testament is modeled in Christ's meeting with _____ (Luke 19:1-10).

    c. This incident gives us important insight into discipling others:

1. Look for the _____

Jesus "was passing through." Discipling events often happen during the _____ _____.

2. Identify the Prospect

"When Jesus reached the spot, he looked up and said to him, 'Zacchaeus . . .'" (Luke 19:5).

    a. Prospects for intentional relationships in discipleship may include:

        (1) Prebelievers who express an _____ in church affiliation

        (2) Prebelievers who have a _____ of church affiliation

        (3) _____ who are just starting their faith journey

        (4) _____ who are struggling with personal or family faith issues

        (5) New _____ who are in need of friendship

        (6) People who have been on a _____

        (7) Small-group attendees who express _____

    b. Intentional relationships are _____ one step at a time.

    c. Your first meeting with a prebeliever or disciple should be more about _____ than making a _____.

    d. Get to know:

        (1) _____ members

        (2) Family _____

        (3) Church _____

        (4) _____

        (5) _____

        (6) _____ (music, books, food, Web sites, etc.)

3. Take Intentional Risks

"'Zacchaeus, come down immediately. I must stay at your house today.' So he came down at once and welcomed him gladly. All the people saw this and began to mutter, 'He has gone to be the guest of a "sinner"'" (Luke 19:5-7).

    a. Jesus risked _____. (An intentional relationship includes willingness to spend the time necessary to let that person know you are sincerely interested in him or her.)

    b. Jesus risked _____. "He has gone to be the guest of a 'sinner.'" Establishing an intentional relationship with another may include going to that person's "turf."

(1) Making a brief appearance at a function

(2) Greeting the person who invited you

(3) And then politely making your exit

c. Jesus risked _____. "Zacchaeus stood up and said to the Lord, 'Look, Lord! Here and now I give half of my possessions to the poor, and if I have cheated anybody out of anything, I will pay back four times the amount'" (Luke 19:8).

d. Jesus risked _____. "Jesus said to him, 'Today salvation has come to this house'" (v. 9a).

e. Jesus risked _____. "This man, too, is a son of Abraham. For the Son of Man came to seek and to save what was lost" (vv. 9b-10).

(1) Prebelievers are often afraid to lose the _____ of family and friends.

(2) You will need to _____ with them.

4. Minister like Jesus

a. Jesus met people at their _____ (Mark 10:51-52).

b. Jesus helped people believe they could become _____ (Matt. 4:19).

c. Jesus pointed _____ of hopeless situations (John 11:21-26).

d. Jesus _____ on people (Luke 22:32).

e. Jesus gave with no _____ (Matt. 16:25).

f. Jesus always encouraged people to _____ (Matt. 5:41).

g. Jesus relied on the _____ (Matt. 4:4).

h. Jesus was always _____ (Luke 2:49).

i. Jesus never compromised His _____ (Matt. 4:9-10).

j. Jesus taught with _____ (Matt. 9:35-36).

k. Jesus lived a life of _____ (Luke 10:21).

l. Jesus prayed _____ (Luke 6:12).

m. Jesus observed people _____ (Mark 12:41).

n. Jesus lived _____ (Matt. 8:20).

o. Jesus forgave without _____ (Matt. 18:21-22).

p. Jesus obeyed the Father _____ (Matt. 26:42).

155

11

Identify Spiritual Understanding Levels
(Student's Guide)

Introduction

Philip the disciple was on a missionary trip when he met a member of Queen Candace's royal court, who was reading the Scriptures. It turned into a discipling ministry: Acts 8:26-40.

(1) He _____ the Spirit's leading (vv. 26-27). God will make the _____; you will need to be open to His Spirit's leading.

(2) He _____ a spiritual understanding level (vv. 30-31). To _____ _____ needed, he had to discover the official's level of spiritual understanding.

(3) He _____ from his level of understanding (vv. 34-35). He discovered an _____ and began to teach accordingly.

(4) He _____ to the next level (vv. 36-38). Help the disciple understand the importance of religious practices in light of being _____ or of being _____.

(5) He _____ him (vv. 39-40). Discipleship has both _____ and _____ dimensions. At the appropriate time, new disciples are trusted to make some _____ on their own—yet remaining on the prayer list and contact list of the discipler.

Levels of Understanding

a. Philip's discipleship encounter teaches about the importance of discerning the _____ of others.

b. As a discipler you will need to know _____.

c. There are at least _____ of spiritual understanding and a proposed teaching path.

  (1) *Level one: the prebeliever*

    Christ himself taught us about reaching out to people in the scriptural account of the meeting with the Samaritan woman at the well (John 4:4-30).

    (a) He established an _____ friendship (vv. 7-9).
- He met the Samaritan at her point of need, no matter the _____.
- Intentional friendship has an end goal of _____. Some conversation starters may include:
  - Religious _____
  - _____ and their relationship to faith
  - _____ about God
  - _____
- Responses will give insights
  - Knowledge of the _____
  - A "_____" (atheistic, agnostic, pluralistic, etc.)
  - Personal or spiritual _____

    (b) He developed an _____ (vv. 10-11). It was merely a link to the more important subject: the condition of _____.

(c) He made a thought-provoking _____ (vv. 16-18). Jesus brought the woman to a point of _____.

(d) He gave her a glimpse of _____ (vv. 23-24). Jesus showed her

_____.

(e) He taught her about _____ of God's Word (v. 26). One-on-one disciple-ship is leading a person to an encounter with the _____

_____.

(2) *Level two: new believer*
   • One who has recently made a decision to _____.
   • The disciple Ananias's spiritual mentoring of Saul (later named Paul) is a gold standard (Acts 9:10-20).

(a) He _____ (vv. 11-13). Ananias had heard about Saul's former lifestyle. But he was compelled by the Holy Spirit to take on the assignment—no matter the personal cost. Discipleship is often costly.

(b) He _____ (v. 17*ab*).
   • Ananias let Saul know they were on _____. Saul's whole world had been turned upside down.
   • Your task as a discipler is to let them know that you are concerned about their

_____.

(c) He _____ (vv. 17*c*-18). Ananias began to explain "the Way" to Saul.
   • He familiarized him with the _____ of the Christian faith.
   • He advised him on Christian _____ and a Christian _____.
   • He encouraged him to use his _____, _____, and _____ in ministry.

(d) He _____ (vv. 19-20).
   • Ananias wasn't _____ by Paul's abilities.
   • Ananias recognized they were God-given, and served God's _____ _____ for the church.

(3) *Uncommitted or unassigned believer*
   (a) You may be asked to encourage more established believers to make a next-level

_____.
      • Small _____
      • Church _____
      • Volunteer _____
      • Mission _____

   (b) You may also be asked to encourage a fellow believer to make a stronger commitment to the local church through _____.

   (c) Aquila and Priscilla were members of the Early Church who made *next-level* commitments (Acts 18:1-26). Paul (formerly Saul) saw they had _____ to be ministers and disciplers and encouraged them toward ministry.
      • He _____ them (vv. 2-3).
      • He _____ them (v. 4).
      • He _____ them (v. 19).

   (d) Your task is not only to teach the new disciples the "principles of flight" but also to en-courage them to "_____."

157

12

Supply a Support System
(Student's Guide)

Introduction

   a. Encouraging the disciple to a next-level commitment takes a _____

   _____.

   b. The basic qualities of _____, _____, _____,
   and _____ must be present in each discipleship assignment.

   c. Those qualities should be present in a _____ for your disciple, no
   matter his or her level of spiritual understanding.

1. New Believer

   The apostle Paul called the disciple Timothy his "_____" in the faith. Discipling a new believer
might be compared to a parent's care for a _____.

   • _____: motor skills, hearing, vision, and
   communication.[17]

   • Those principles are seen in the apostle Paul's _____ for his disciples:

      a. _____: **building movement and coordination** (Col. 1:9-12).

         (1) He prayed for their growth in _____ (v. 9). He prayed that the Holy
         Spirit would _____ on their minds. Sup-
         ply your disciple with a support system of _____. Guidelines:
         • Don't be afraid of _____.
         • Don't be _____ by personal issues.
         • Don't assume that your student knows how to _____

         _____.
         • Don't tackle the "_____."
         • Don't _____ (Isa. 55:11).

         (2) He prayed for their growth in _____ (Col. 1:10).
         • Paul was concerned that Christians be _____

         _____.

         • Paul prayed that his disciples would _____.

         (3) He prayed for their _____ (vv. 11-12).
         • Be _____.
         • Point out the _____.
         • Remind them of the _____: heaven.

      b. _____: **Responding to voices and other sounds** (2 Cor. 13:7-9).
      Paul wanted his disciples to trust in _____, not human effort.
         • Provide your disciple with a support system of _____

         _____.

            • God never speaks contrary to _____.
            • God never leads contrary to _____.
            • God uses the _____.
            • God can even use _____ to strengthen the disciple.

         (1) Your availability when your disciple is facing tempting times will be a great source of

         _____.

         (2) Let your disciple know _____.

(3) Encourage your disciple to a life of _____.
   - Provide literature and a study that will teach about _____

   _____.

   - Share your testimony of how you discovered the power of _____

   _____.

c. _____: **Learning to focus** (Eph. 1:18-21).
   - Paul was a _____ man (Phil. 3:13-14).
   - He encouraged those whom he led to focus their attention on the future _____

   _____.

   (1) He prayed that they would be people of a _____ (Eph. 1:18*a*). Help
   your disciple learn how to _____.

   (2) He prayed that they would know about _____ (v. 18*b*). Make a dif-
   ference in your disciple's worldview:
   - Teach about God's _____.
   - Teach about _____ to God.
   - Teach about the principle of _____.
   - Teach about the hope of _____.
   - Teach about investments of _____.

   (3) He prayed that they would understand _____ (vv. 19*b*-21*a*).
   Teach your disciple about end time hope.

d. _____: **expressing affection** (Phil. 1:9-11).
   - Paul was concerned that disciples understood the depths of commitment and interdependence that come with being a part of _____.
   - Christianity includes the _____ as well as the will. Guide the disciple in making wise decisions regarding _____.

2. Newly Committed Believer

The discipler is also a _____: provides training and guidance for committed believers who have
taken next-level steps of growth or ministry.

   a. Try to determine the disciple's level of _____.

   b. Evaluate the disciple's _____.

   c. Observe _____.

   d. Evaluate the disciple's _____.

You will multiply your own ministry many times over through the dedicated service
of one in whom you have invested your life.

13

Contact Regarding Spiritual Progress/Needs
(Student's Guide)

Introduction

In emergency care there is a window of time known as the golden hour, where patients under treatment have the greatest likelihood of _____.

1. Golden Hour Contacts

a. There is a _____, a golden hour, when focused care is crucial to the spiritual survival of the disciple or when the desired spiritual effect is best achieved.

b. The golden hour is an accumulated _____ of focused contact time each week.

c. Several _____ may be included in the golden hour contact time:
- _____
- _____ (and instant message)
- _____
- _____
- _____

2. Contact Protocol

a. Build a quality _____.

b. Anything that is said to be "_____" should be exactly that.

c. Keep the relationship _____.

d. Make sure the contacts have _____.

e. Use the type of contact that _____.

f. Make sure the contact has an _____ of spiritual growth.

3. Contact Methods

a. Telephone call
   (1) Make sure a telephone call is _____.
   (2) Make brevity your _____.
       (a) Express your _____.
       (b) Check on _____.
       (c) Strengthen an _____ relationship.
   (3) Prayerfully think about _____.
   (4) Make it a _____ call.
   (5) Make it a _____ call.
       (a) Listen for the _____.
       (b) Respond according to the _____.
       (c) List _____.
       (d) Pick out and quote an _____.
       (e) Discuss a book, chapter, or verse from the Bible that _____
       _____.
       (f) Remind your disciple that you are continually _____
       _____.

b. E-mail or text messaging
  (1) E-mail
    (a) Use _____ rather than business address.
    (b) Don't "_____" message to others.
    (c) Prayerfully think about the _____.
    (d) Make the message _____.
    (e) Be _____.
    (f) Be _____.
    (g) Limit the e-mails to _____ each week.
    (h) Avoid including or attaching "_____" content.
    (i) Include a _____.
    (j) Check for _____.
    (k) Remind your disciple of your _____.
    (l) Remind your disciple of your _____.
  (2) Text messages
    (a) Avoid "_____" content.
    (b) Get right to the _____.
    (c) Remind your disciple of your _____.
    (d) Include a Scripture _____ rather than an entire verse (e.g., John 3:16).
    (e) Be _____.
    (f) Limit the _____ of messages.
  (3) Instant messages (IM) or video conferencing

c. Note or card
  (1) Use notes or cards for encouraging or recognizing a _____.
  (2) _____ and strengthening.
  (3) Time of _____.
  (4) Reinforce _____.
  (5) Give _____.
  (6) _____ milestone.
  (7) Recognize an _____.

d. Personal appointment
  (1) Some of Jesus' most memorable discipling was _____:
    (a) Nicodemus
    (b) Zacchaeus
    (c) Peter
    (d) Mary and Martha
  (2) Guidelines:
    (a) Set a time that will be _____.
    (b) Determine to meet within _____ parameters.
    (c) Avoid disrupting family or work _____.
    (d) Avoid conflicting with church _____.
    (e) Send a _____.
    (f) Pick up the _____ (restaurant meetings).
    (g) Make a _____ contact.
  (3) Include:
    (a) _____
    (b) Praise for _____
    (c) _____ or needs
    (d) _____

161

(e) Inquiry into personal or family _____

(f) Church _____ reminders

(g) Brief _____

(h) Bible _____

4. Making the Golden Hour Golden

a. _____ or changing directions

_____ that the discipling effort can be scaled back or change directions:

(1) The disciple is making obvious _____.

(2) The relationship has a different _____.

(3) The disciple has reached a "_____" level.

b. _____ discipling effectiveness

(1) Keep your _____ in mind.

(2) Stay _____.

(3) Know your _____.

14

Incorporate into the Life and Ministries of the Church
(Student's Guide)

Introduction

a. New disciples need the _____ of a local church (Heb. 10:25).

  (1) Some have _____ attended church.

    (a) Speak _____ of your own church background.

    (b) Include a study of the _____ in your discipling.

    (c) Invite them to be your guests for a _____, followed by a fellowship time.

    (d) Encourage them to take a _____ or _____ class.

    (e) Reinforce the importance of making a _____ of their new faith commitment.

    (f) Reinforce the importance of worshipping with _____, including the reading and study of _____ in a structured environment.

  (2) Some have _____ by the church.

    (a) _____ to their opinions and attitudes of the church.

    (b) _____ of your own church background.

    (c) Introduce them to _____, positive role models in the church.

  (3) Some have _____ the church.

    (a) Listen sympathetically to _____.

    (b) _____ of your own church background.

    (c) Reinforce the _____ with other believers, including the reading and study of the Bible in a structured environment.

    (d) _____ to a worship service as your guests, followed by a fellowship time.

    (e) Reinforce the necessity of _____ as an outworking of their faith.

b. Incorporating the new disciple into the life and ministries of the church can be done at several important "_____."

1. Baptism and the Lord's Supper

a. _____

  Action Plan: _____ the disciple's scheduled baptism (plan a fellowship time, including providing refreshments, following the baptismal service and child care during and after the ceremony).

b. _____

  Action Plan

  (1) Discuss the _____ of the Lord's Supper observance.

  (2) Sit with the disciple and _____.

2. Worship Event

Action Plan

a. Discuss the need for _____ and private worship.

b. Invite them (along with their friends and family) to _____ _____.

c. Introduce them to other _____ (especially age-/interest-related attendees).

    d. Make sure they have a _____ and church _____.

    e. Invite them to _____ following the service.

3. Special Event

    a. Events

        (1) Christmas and Easter _____

        (2) _____

        (3) Church _____ celebrations

        (4) _____

        (5) Church _____

        (6) _____

        (7) Missions _____

        (8) _____

    b. Action Plan

        (1) Invite and _____ the disciple of the event.

        (2) Explain the _____ of the event, including sending advertising.

        (3) Assist with _____.

        (4) Give _____.

        (5) Plan a follow-up meeting or fellowship time

            _____

            _____, inviting other attendees, members, and church staff.

        (6) Encourage _____ for the next event.

4. Small Group

    a. Groups

        (1) _____

        (2) _____

        (3) _____

    b. Action Plan

        (1) _____ the disciple about the group meeting.

        (2) Explain the _____ of the small group.

        (3) Provide _____.

        (4) Deflect questions to the disciple that would make the disciple uncomfortable by

            _____ or answering them in

            a _____ way.

        (5) Give the disciple an opportunity to _____ a small group.

        (6) Encourage _____ in set-up or teaching (when appropriate).

        (7) Schedule a _____ that will include the disciple and other group members.

5. Interest Group

    Action Plan

    a. Provide _____ about the interest group, including map directions, times, locations.

    b. _____ the disciple to other group members.

c. _____ group special events that include your disciple (musicals, drama, sporting events).

d. _____ disciples of your prayers regarding their participation.

6. Ministry Team

Action Plan

a. Pray for your disciple's ministry _____.

b. Provide information on ministry _____.

c. Alert ministry team _____ of your disciple's interests and abilities.

d. _____ your disciple toward a team.

e. Offer to be a _____.

f. Help provide _____ for team events.

15

Pray Daily for Spiritual Growth
(Student's Guide)

Introduction

    a. Disciples need a _____ team.

    b. Prayer is a _____ of warfare (Eph. 6:12).

    c. Christian living is a _____ effort (1 Cor. 12:12).

    d. Prayer is a form of spiritual _____.

1. Interdependence

    a. Pray for your disciple's _____.

    b. Pray for your disciple's _____ to the Holy Spirit's guidance.

    c. Pray for your disciple's _____ times.

    d. Pray that your disciple will pursue _____.

    e. Pray that your disciple will _____ others for Christ.

2. Prayer Partnerships

    a. Two or more believers may _____ to pray for prebelievers, new believers, or other believers.

    b. Biblical history proves there is _____:

        (1) Two _____ were called to be disciples (Matt. 4:18, 21).

        (2) Two _____ were sent to prepare for Jesus' entrance into Jerusalem (Matt. 21:1-3).

        (3) Disciples were sent out to minister _____ (Mark 6:7).

        (4) Seventy disciples were sent out to minister _____ (Luke 10:1).

"Again I say to you that if two of you agree on earth concerning anything that they ask, it will be done for them by My Father in heaven" (Matt. 18:19, NKJV).

    c. Prayer partners

        (1) Strengthen individual _____

        (2) Help to offset individual _____

        (3) Keep each other _____

        (4) Remind each other of prayer _____

        (5) Widen the area of _____

    d. Prayer partnerships are _____.

    e. Prayer partnerships may be used _____ to individual prayer.

        (1) What is a prayer partnership?

            (a) An _____ between two or more people to pray daily

            (b) For _____ on their _____

            (c) For a specified _____

            (d) In agreement with _____

        (2) What do prayer partners do?

           Prayer partners _____ either in person, by phone, or by other appropriate means (e.g., video conferencing).

(3) **How should prayer partnerships be formed?**

    (a) Prayer partnerships may be formed from an _____ prayer effort, such as prayer cells or big brothers/big sisters discipling ministries.

    (b) Prayer partnerships may be formed from _____ or _____ within the church.

(4) **What are the qualifications of a prayer partner?**

    (a) Complete a _____ or discipleship course

    (b) Complete a prayer partner _____

    (c) Active in the _____ (preferably members)

    (d) Disciples who have a _____

    (e) Able to keep _____

    (f) Known for _____

    (g) Of the same _____

(5) **When and where should prayer partners meet?**

    Prayer partners should plan to meet at least _____ each week.

(6) **What should be included in prayer partner meetings?**

    (a) Sharing _____ regarding prayer or faith

    (b) Sharing of prayer concerns from the _____

    (c) Mutual _____

    (d) _____ for the other prayer partner

    (e) _____ for answered prayer

(7) **Who should the prayer partners pray for?**

    (a) Primarily the _____ of a prebeliever, new believer, or other believers.

    (b) Other _____ may be provided by the prayer coordinator, a pastoral staff member, or from big brothers/big sisters or prayer cells.

(8) **How long should a prayer partnership last?**

    (a) Some will _____ for a long period of time.

    (b) Some will form a prayer partnership for an _____ _____.

    (c) The length of time depends on such factors as:

        • The _____ of the prayer partners

        • The _____ of the need

        • The _____ of staff, friends, or family

        • The _____ to a prayer concern

(9) **How can prayer partnerships be multiplied?**

    • As _____ to the prayer partners and to the congregation (including answered prayer from your own discipling effort), enthusiasm will begin to build for prayer partnerships.

    • _____ of new faith commitments may be part of a public worship service.

    (a) _____ that new prayer partnerships will soon be formed.

        • Launch a three- to four-week _____ or short-term _____ on prayer.

        • Include _____ on prayer and faith in print publications or electronic announcements.

        • Announce _____ to prayer in worship services or small-group meetings.

        • Include _____ on prayer in worship services.

        • Place _____ that includes Bible verses or quotes about prayer in high-traffic areas of the church or meeting place.

- Have one or more _____ write a 50- to 100-word _____ on what prayer partnerships have meant to them (letting them know in advance that the article may be edited for word count and content).

(b) Organize a _____ prayer partnerships _____ class.

(c) _____ the prayer partnerships class (120 minutes).
- Session 1: How to Pray for Others (intercessory prayer) (30 minutes)
- Break (10 minutes)
- Session 2: The Duties of a Prayer Partner (amplified lesson from the "Duties of a Prayer Partner" handout) (30 minutes)
- Form prayer partnerships (20 minutes)
  - Ask for _____ partnerships.
  - _____ partnerships.
  - Have the prayer partners _____ for brief prayer time.

(d) _____ prayer partners in a worship service or meeting. Have congregation members _____ prayer requests on prayer request cards.

(e) _____ prayer requests in a post-service event meeting.
- Compile _____ lists on prayer list cards.
- Place the _____ in church stationery envelopes.
- Distribute _____ to prayer partnerships.
- _____ encouragement and instruction.
- Close in _____.

Remember the words of Jesus to His disciple: "I have prayed for you . . . that your faith may not fail" (Luke 22:32).

16

Look for Spiritual Gifts
(Student's Guide)

Introduction

a. _____ and _____ are part of God's master design (Eph. 4:11-16).

b. Abilities and personalities surrendered fully to Jesus Christ are _____ through which He reaches the lost and strengthens His church (Acts 1:8).

1. What Are the Differences Between the *Fruit* of the Spirit and the *Gifts* of the Spirit?

Fruit

1. Defines what a Christian _____
2. _____ in every Christian
3. _____
4. Satan _____ imitate
5. Deals with _____
6. _____ in itself
7. _____
8. According to _____ _____

Gifts

1. Determines what a Christian _____
2. _____ in each Christian
3. _____
4. Satan _____ imitate
5. Deals with _____
6. _____ to an end
7. _____
8. _____ to spirituality

2. What Is a Spiritual Gift?

a. Spiritual gifts are divinely enabled _____.

b. Spiritual gifts are used in helping to fulfill Christ's _____.

c. Believers should seek to discover what Spirit-enabled abilities they may possess. How?

   (1) Identify _____ that support Christ's mission.

   (2) Identify natural _____ that would fulfill that interest.

   (3) _____ on how those interests and talents may be used for Christ.

   (4) Look for _____ to utilize interests and talents in mission supporting efforts.

d. The greatest gift is the _____ (Acts 2:15-17).

3. To Whom Are Spiritual Gifts Given?

a. Spiritual gifts are given to _____ (1 Cor. 12:7).

b. Spiritual gifts are "activated" or "released" when a person is _____ _____ (1 Cor. 12:13).

c. The Holy Spirit, the giver of spiritual gifts, _____ the new believer (Acts 2:38).

d. Believers do not "_____" their gifts. They are given to them by Christ in accordance with His will (1 Cor. 12:11).

e. No one believer has all of _____, nor is any one gift common to all.

4. What Is the Purpose of Spiritual Gifts?

Spiritual gifts help fulfill the broader, eternal scope of God's promises.

a. They _____: "To prepare God's people for works of service" (Eph. 4:12*a*). They also are "_____" used to

(1) _____ the good news of the gospel to prebelievers

(2) _____ and enlighten believers by the Word of God

(3) _____ the church into a functioning body

(4) _____ the church in accomplishing growth

b. They _____: "So that the body of Christ may be built up" (v. 12*b*).

c. They _____: "Until we all reach unity in the faith and in the knowledge of the Son of God" (v. 13*a*).

d. They _____: "Become mature, attaining to the whole measure of the fullness of Christ" (v. 13*b*).

e. They _____: "Then we will no longer be infants, tossed back and forth by the waves, and blown here and there by every wind of teaching and by the cunning and craftiness of men in their deceitful scheming. Instead, speaking the truth in love, we will in all things grow up into him who is the Head, that is, Christ" (vv. 14-15).

f. They _____: "From him the whole body, joined and held together by every supporting ligament, grows and builds itself up in love, as each part does its work" (v. 16).

5. How Do *Human Talents* and Spiritual *Gifts* Differ?

a. Abilities are the _____ that God blesses and empowers to accomplish His eternal purpose.

b. Distributed and anointed by the Holy Spirit, they are _____ through their dedication to Christ and His cause.

(1) One spiritual gift is not _____ than another.

(2) They are not to be used as personal _____.

(3) They are to be used to bring attention to _____.

(4) They should not be at the source of _____ between believers; they should be a source of _____.

Talents	Gifts
1. _____ from forefathers	1. Given by the _____
2. Present from _____	2. Present from _____
3. God-given to _____ members of the human race	3. God-given to members of _____
4. For _____ activities	_____
5. Can be operated _____ of the Holy Spirit	4. For ministry of the _____
6. Ministers primarily on a _____ level	5. _____ on the Holy Spirit
7. Effects are usually _____	6. Ministers on a _____ level
8. Glorifies _____	7. Effects are _____
	8. Glorifies _____

6. Discovering Spiritual Gifts

Helping disciples discover abilities that may be used in Kingdom-building is essential to their _____ and the _____.

a. Introduce them to a spiritual gifts _____.

b. _____ the abilities that could be used in the church.

c. Make their discovery of their spiritual gifts a matter of _____.

d. Help them see how a _____ will bring wholeness—and holiness—to their spiritual journey.

17

Enlist in Ministry
(Student's Guide)

Introduction

    a. Nowhere does the "light" of a disciple's life bring a warmer and brighter glow than through the _____ of the church (1 Cor. 12:27-31).

    b. You are the _____ who will teach your disciples how to take an active part in church ministry.

        (1) Through _____

        (2) Through _____ with another

        (3) Through _____ to a specific position

        (4) Through _____ another

        (5) Through _____ ministries

        (6) Through _____

    Not only will you encourage them to find a place of ministry, but you will also guide them in enlisting in that ministry—always in cooperation with the leadership of the church.

1. Local Church Ministry

    a. The church is "organizational machinery" that needs both _____.

    b. The "parts" make the machinery _____, while the "labor" keeps it _____! And the Holy Spirit's presence and power keeps it _____.

    c. There is a place for your disciple's interest and ability.

        (1) List the _____ of ministries.

        (2) Consult with local church leadership about needed _____.

        (3) Ask local church leadership to supply _____ for volunteer needs.

        (4) _____ your disciple's ability and experience.

        (5) Match _____ with volunteer needs.

        (6) _____ your disciple with volunteer possibilities.

        (7) Recommend a volunteer _____.

2. Missions Ministry

    a. The church also has a _____ (Luke 10:1-2).

    b. Spiritual mentoring can encourage your disciple to have a "_____."

        (1) Teach them about Christ's global _____.

        (2) Share missions _____ with them.

        (3) Invite them to assist with a missions _____.

        (4) Tell them how your _____ involvement has benefited you.

        (5) Encourage them to participate in a missions _____.

        (6) Encourage _____ for or with overseas missionaries.

        (7) Encourage them to be _____ with an overseas missionary.

        (8) Encourage them to _____ a mission or missionary.

        (9) Inform them of _____ missions opportunities.

(10) Teach them about _____ missions ministry (short-term or vocational missions opportunity).

3. Compassionate Ministry

a. Your disciples must understand that their own _____ is a mission field.

b. Enlisting them in _____ is a great place to start.

c. Compassionate ministries minister to the whole person—_____,
_____, _____, _____, and
_____.

d. Disciples' experiences with compassionate ministries may be just the beginning of a _____ ministry—including _____ ministry.

   (1) Study compassionate ministries in the _____.

   (2) Acquaint them with ministry _____ in the community.

   (3) Ask them to _____ with a compassionate ministry on-site.

   (4) Introduce them to community compassionate ministries _____.

   (5) Inform them of _____ compassionate ministries.

4. Small-Group Ministry

a. Small groups, such as a neighborhood Bible studies, big brothers/big sisters or prayer cells is an exciting _____ to ministry.

b. Small groups are good _____ grounds.

c. Working in a small group setting usually builds _____.

d. Training and supervision provide a _____.

e. Encourage volunteerism in small groups as a way of enriching _____ _____ and utilizing _____.

5. Event Ministry

a. Special events offer both the discipler and the disciple a time of _____ and hands-on
_____.

b. Your disciple will see _____.

PRAYER CELLS
(Discipling Plan)

Aggressive church multiplication usually starts small—in small groups. From the apostles' first orientation, to their farewell meeting before His ascension, big things happened when their small group got together with Jesus. And big things still happen when Christ's disciples get together with Him! "Where two or three come together in my name, there am I with them" (Matt. 18:20).

Soul-winning plans, like Each One Win One, play an important part in releasing the spiritual skills of believers to impact communities for Christ in a first wave effort. But what's next? We sing "Onward, Christian Soldiers," but how does the army of Christ keep going? One effective way is to regroup for prayer. Prayer is the Church's greatest weapon. The spiritual power of supplication and intercession strengthens Christ's followers and enlarges their influence, which is what the early believers quickly discovered: "With great power the apostles continued to testify to the resurrection of the Lord Jesus, and much grace was upon them all" (Acts 4:33).

The church's goal shouldn't be maintenance but maximum growth, developing healthy churches that will duplicate themselves in vibrant church plants and, in turn, impact neighborhoods, regions, and entire countries. Prayer cells have been used by God throughout time to do just that. For example, prayer cells will not only build the mother church that launches them but also let her reach out and start new congregations—building the Kingdom church by church.

Jim Dorsey, director of NewStart in the Church of the Nazarene, often states that the Church's studies show that "the increase in number of churches was a significant factor in the denomination's growth." Paul Orjala shared at a missions conference that the Church "owes its record of rapid growth more to rapid church planting than to any other factor. . . . As we plant more churches, the result will be a dramatic increase in our overall growth rate." In fact, the only way we will impact the world, and fulfill the Great Commission, is by planting new churches.

So through a simple system of prayer cells people can be won to Christ, new leaders can be trained and called to preach, and new churches can be started. The prayer cell plan is designed to enable and encourage natural church growth. The successful result has been seen countless times in new, self-supporting churches. The Church of the Nazarene is using this method to multiply churches throughout the world.

The Purpose of Prayer Cells

The purpose of prayer cells is, first of all, to pray. There is power in prayer—personal prayer and corporate prayer. The group dynamic of a prayer cell brings people together in spirit and purpose and sends them out with hearts afire. When two of the apostles were released from the persecutor's prison, they went immediately to a prayer cell:

> On their release, Peter and John went back to their own people and reported all that the chief priests and elders had said to them. When they heard this, they raised their voices together in prayer. . . . "Now, Lord, consider their threats and enable your servants to speak your word with great boldness. Stretch out your hand to heal and perform miraculous signs and wonders through the name of your holy servant Jesus." After they prayed, the place where they were meeting was shaken. And they were all filled with the Holy Spirit and spoke the word of God boldly *(Acts 4:23-24, 29-31).*

And the rest is history.

At an appointed time, for an agreed period of time, people meet together to pray for others—especially for the needs of the unchurched. Does it work? It has been discovered that about 90 percent of the prayer requests are answered by the end of each cycle of prayer cells!

Second, the purpose of prayer cells is to increase the Kingdom. As people begin to see answers to prayer in their lives, they become more open to the gospel and to the church. Established churches (mother churches) start prayer cells to reach beyond their four walls to the community—and grow in the process themselves! They grow in leadership, creating a greater support system. They grow in fellowship, inviting new people into their congregations. And they grow numerically, seeing new believers won into the Kingdom. Also, the prayer cells develop naturally into organized churches, giving the mother church a chance to decentralize and to multiply its ministry.

The Biblical Basis for Prayer Cells

Once again, the Early Church modeled the best methods for aggressive church multiplication. Where did it start? Where did the organized church begin to take its earthly form? It took its earthy form in homes and in small groups: "They broke bread in their homes and ate together with glad and sincere hearts" (Acts 2:46). Their house meetings blossomed into organized churches.

The impact was phenomenal! God promises to reveal His plans to those who pray: "Call to me and I will answer you and tell you great and unsearchable things you do not know" (Jer. 33:3). The result of that spiritual dependence is seen in the life of the Early Church. Acts 16:5 says, "The churches were strengthened in the faith and grew daily in numbers."

This was made possible through small groups that evolved into new congregations, in the power of the Spirit. We believe that this not only can happen again but is happening right now! In South America, the power of the movement that is taking place comes exclusively from prayer. Their planning begins, continues, and ends with prayer. One pastor from the area commented that it was the first time he had seen evangelism and prayer combined in such an intricate way.

Strategies for Starting Prayer Cells

Before a pastor begins any prayer cell strategies, he or she should ask several questions: (1) How many cells should be started? (2) In what types of homes should the cells be started? (3) Where should each cell be started?

1. How Many?

It is best to begin with three or four prayer cells. First, if a church begins with only one cell, and that cell doesn't succeed, it may look as if the whole plan is doomed to failure. Second, it is easier to build enthusiasm with a larger number of cells. (However, it is usually not wise to begin with more than four, because it is more difficult to establish and evaluate that many cells.)

The goal should be to reach a point where there is a prayer cell for every 10 members. As the plan progresses, and there are more trained leaders, it is possible to manage a larger number of cells. In São Paulo, for instance, when the district had 400 members, 40 prayer cells were established. When the membership reached 600, there were 60 prayer cells. When there were 1,000 members, there were 100 prayer cells functioning.

2. In What Types of Homes?

It's advisable to begin the first prayer cells in the homes of believers. Since you are preparing an initial leadership team, it is important to look for homes where an assortment of religious doctrines is not prevalent.

Soon the cells will multiply, and then you can include homes with only one or two believers in the family. In some cases, a prayer cell may even be held in a home without any believers at all.

In one city, where the church launched a major evangelistic thrust, there were 300 members in 50 homes. Prayer cells were begun in the homes of 17 believers. Three years later, there were prayer cells in 150 homes, with 90 of those homes opening for prayer cells because *unconverted* family members had become Christians.

However, as recommended, the first leaders were trained in the homes of believers. Once they had training and experience, cells were established where only some of the members were believers. And in some cases unbelievers opened their homes because they were curious about the Christian faith. Opening cells in the homes of unbelievers usually happened only after prayer cell leaders had six to nine months of training and experience and were spiritually strong.

Targeted prayer cell sites may be classified by colors in a file, or on a map, showing
  • Those where *all* persons in the home are believers

- Those where *some* persons in the home are believers
- Those where there is only *one* believer in the home
- Those where there are *sympathizers, visitors, or friends* of the church

3. Where to Meet?

It's best to locate the cells in a place where a new church could be planted. It should be a place large enough for several families and in a home where the host family is willing to make a long-term commitment to a prayer cell—and possibly to a mission or baby church. Consideration should also be given to the distance from the mother church, the location of other cells, and the proximity to the congregation's members. It helps to pinpoint the targeted area on a map, calculating the distance between the homes and the church. (Note the distance on the map in blocks or miles.)

Since one of the purposes of prayer cells is to promote the growth of the mother church, prayer cells may be anywhere from 50 yards to 10 miles from it. Distance is not a problem. There are people who will not attend a church even if they live on the same block with it. However, they may make contact with the church through a prayer cell.

If there are enough believers in the area, two or three cells may exist a short distance apart without a problem. This will even increase the possibility of opening a mission, especially when celebration services are held in three cells. Though not all prayer cells become missions, experience tells us that out of every 10 cells, 3 become missions and that out of every 10 missions, 3 become organized churches.

What Happens in the Prayer Cells?

Prayer cells have several important things in common. The personalities of the cell group members may vary along with the styles and characteristics of the homes, but the prayer cells follow a common organizational pattern.

The Agenda

A prayer cell is a weekly meeting that lasts between 45 minutes to an hour. While a prayer cell agenda is not complicated, attention should be given to the proper functioning of the cell. It consists of three activities: (1) testimonies and songs of praise, (2) a chapter reading from the Book of Acts, and (3) a prayer time. Prayer is the key that makes the cell evangelistic. Each person prays—especially focusing on the spiritual needs of the unconverted. (If we only pray for believers, we have merely substituted a house, a little salt shaker, for a church building, a bigger salt shaker.) The purpose for meeting in homes is twofold: to give believers closer proximity to the unconverted and to decentralize the local church.

At a later time, prayer cell members can communicate to the unconverted that they are praying for them. This will provide a natural opportunity to invite them to the prayer cell meeting house to hear the gospel presented.

The Leaders

Prayer cells without leadership can turn into *gossip sessions with refreshments*. Trained leadership is essential to the purpose, planning, and program of the prayer cell strategy, but the plan is designed to include those who lack previous leadership experience.

There are three key leaders in every cell. They take turns leading the group, reading the Bible chapter, and writing the prayer requests in a notebook. As they rotate responsibilities each week, they will gain valuable leadership experience.

Each leader can then train two other prayer cell leaders. This will allow each cell to multiply into three cells at the end of each cycle.

The prayer cell leaders' responsibilities are as follows:

The first leader is responsible for directing the meeting. He or she will bring the group to order and lead a time of testimony and singing.

The second leader will read one chapter from the Book of Acts. (This section of the Bible is filled with church growth and Christian fellowship principles, and it also reminds cell groups of how early Christians met in house churches.)

175

The third leader leads the cell in prayer and keeps the prayer cell notebook. He or she records the following information:

1. Prayer requests (including those for personal needs, family members, acquaintances, and—always—the unconverted).
2. A corresponding number for each prayer request. (It is important to know how many requests there are so the number of answered prayers can be calculated later.)
3. The date of each prayer request.
4. Names, addresses, and other observations about the unconverted for whom prayers are being offered (necessary information so these persons can be invited to the evangelistic campaign).
5. Dates of answered prayers (underline the corresponding recorded prayer requests). The person who made the request should provide this information when the answer is received.
6. The chapter from the Book of Acts read in the cell group meeting that week.

What to Avoid

The success of the cell group hinges on proven principles derived from the experience of those who have been involved in its strategy. Here are some suggestions for effective prayer cell groups.

The Cells Should Not Include Preaching or In-Depth Bible Study

Preaching or in-depth Bible study would limit the number of prayer cells. Many local churches do not have those who are qualified to preach, other than the pastor. If they were to depend on preachers to lead prayer cells, they would restrict the number of cells to the number of available preachers.

Also, these activities would limit the participation of believers who desire to be a part of the prayer cell ministry but are not gifted in preaching or teaching.

Leadership Should Not Come from Any Church but the Mother Church

Leaders from other churches could create issues about biblical doctrines and, later on, cause complications when the time comes to form a mission or new church.

Also, unconverted persons should not be prayer cell leaders. They wouldn't be familiar with the purpose of the cell.

Food or Refreshments Should Not Be Served

The preparation of refreshments puts an extra responsibility on the hosts and limits the multiplication of prayer cells because of the expected work. The objective is to pray, not eat.

The Meeting Should Not Last Longer than 45 Minutes to an Hour

Most prayer cell members work during the day, and if the meeting is too long, they likely will not attend the following week. The leaders should develop the skill of drawing the prayer cell to a close. Perhaps using a familiar line, such as, "This has been a great time of fellowship and prayer. I know we'll be looking forward to next week's meeting."

The Three Leaders Should Not Belong to Any Other Prayer Cell

Burnout is not only a hazard for vocational ministers but common among the laity as well. To avoid overload, the leaders' participation should be limited to one prayer cell. In addition, leadership issues may arise if the leaders of one cell start attending another.

Prayer Requests Should Not Be Focused on Believers' Needs Alone

Those who have been Christians for several years tend to be acquainted with more believers than unbelievers. The members of the cells must make an effort to reach out and to discover the needs of their unchurched friends. The prayer cell should avoid being member-centered. Certainly the church is to follow the advice of the apostle Paul: "Carry each other's burdens, and in this way you will fulfill the law of Christ" (Gal. 6:2). The fellowship that is expressed in times of prayer is one that strengthens the believer. But the primary purpose of the prayer cell is to focus on expanding the Kingdom, not maintaining it.

The Unconverted Should Not Be Invited

There will be a time and place when the unconverted will receive a very important invitation—to be a part of an evangelistic campaign. The prayer cell is a place where the foundation for that campaign is laid. The Bible says, "The man without the Spirit does not accept the things that come from the Spirit of God, for they are foolishness to him, and he cannot understand them, because they are spiritually discerned" (1 Cor. 2:14). Unconverted persons may not only feel uncomfortable in the prayer cell atmosphere but also not understand its purpose. At the end of the three-month cycle, they will be invited to participate in a setting where the simple claims of the gospel will be presented.

Who Is Targeted?

The Pastor Must Encourage Every Believer in the Mother Church to Join a Prayer Cell

The cells should be promoted constantly—from the pulpit, in the church's publications, and individually. Enthusiasm is the foundation for participation in any event, and prayer cells are no exception.

The Pastor Should Watch for Members of the Congregation Who Are Gifted in Prayer Cell Leadership

Watch for those who have demonstrated Christ in their world, are members of the local church, have leadership traits, and have an obvious desire to work.

Caution Should Be Used in Selecting Core Leadership

Among that "80 percent" of the members in most congregations who need to be involved in a ministry, such as the prayer cell, there are three basic personality types: (1) the positive, (2) the negative, and (3) the indifferent. Prayer cells need positive leadership. This next caution is also important: The established leadership of the church may have all of the qualifications—including a positive outlook—but they may have other issues. They may be bound by tradition, for instance. In that case, another search should be started. Qualified and positive leaders may be sought from newer members of the church.

Prayer Cell Leaders Should Come from the Membership of the Church

They may not be experienced, and they may not be trained in leadership principles, but potential prayer cell group leaders should be chosen from those who have proven their loyalty to Christ and to His kingdom by being committed members of a local church.

The Pastor Is Primary in Developing Leadership for the Prayer Cells

He or she chooses the leaders, trains them, and assigns them to their respective cells. The pastor must not delegate this action to another, because these new leaders are the pastor's disciples, so to speak. He or she personally invited them, as the Lord Jesus invited His own disciples, to accomplish a task that will result in the building of the Kingdom.

How Is Leadership Expanded?

Just as the watchmaker learns a trade by working with watches, and the carpenter by working with wood, the prayer cell leader learns by leading a cell. The leader begins to learn how to work with people, learns how to be responsible for a prayer cell, and learns to discover and use spiritual gifts. In fact, the leader can begin a lifelong ministry, preparing for other ministries while leading the cell.

The Role of the Pastor

All through this process, the pastor must stay in close contact with the leaders in training. If problems or disagreements arise, the pastor must be alert to observe every detail and to analyze the true nature of the disagreement. He or she should try to solve problems quickly so that discouragement among other leaders is avoided.

Group dynamics are very important to maintaining enthusiasm among the prayer cell leadership. The pastor will do everything possible to *encourage* the leaders. Pastors must also discipline the leaders, insisting on *commitment,* otherwise discouragement and negative attitudes will follow.

Discovering the Commitment of Leaders

The pastor will undoubtedly have to deal with some prayer cell leaders who are not committed. This is a time of training and testing. The pastor should be on the alert for signs that a prayer cell leader is not fulfilling his or her responsibilities. Tardiness, lack of organization, or a lack of preparation are key indicators. In a spirit of Christian love, the pastor should discuss the leader's responsibilities with the leader, reminding him or her of the covenant that was made in the beginning. The leader should also be reminded that his or her first allegiance is to Christ—and to the building of Christ's kingdom.

It is advisable that the host of the home where a cell group meets not be the leader of that cell. It would be more advisable for a leader to preside over a cell in another home—even a home in another area. It is actually better when a leader lives in another neighborhood. It may be more inconvenient, but it develops discipline that helps to prepare the leader.

Multiplying Leaders

Where there are three leaders, and each performs a different task, they are training each other. After the first cycle, the three leaders may be separated. One may stay in the same house and help train two new leaders. The other two may go to different homes and help train two more leaders in each home. In this way, not only cells but also leaders are multiplied.

At the end of the second cycle, there will be three cells led by the original three leaders, plus six new leaders. The multiplication continues so that after each cycle, each leader takes the responsibility of discipling two new leaders, teaching them what he or she has learned.

Finally, when the pastor divides the leaders among the cells, he or she should try to have one man and two women or vice versa. If a husband and wife are leaders, they should always be in the same cell.

The Discipleship Cell (The Mother Cell)

The foundation of the prayer cell system is the *discipleship cell*. This cell is comprised of all prayer cell leaders, along with the pastor. Its purpose is to give inspiration, guidance, and motivation to the leaders.

This may be the most important meeting in the pastor's week. It is the time when the pastor disciples the leaders. There are five elements in the discipleship process, and each of these should be included in the meetings.

1. The Leaders Should Be Given Solid Spiritual Food Through Bible Study

This will not only help them develop spiritual depth but will also give them an understanding of the church's biblical mission.

2. Prayer Cell Strategies Should Be Taught

The leaders need to understand the purpose and procedures of prayer cells, the rotation of responsibilities, the use of the notebook, and ways that the cells can influence the establishing of a mission, or even the planting of a new church.

3. The Leaders Should Be Motivated to Carry Out the Church's Mission

They must understand the importance of what they are doing in the context of the overall mission of the mother church. Encouragement and praise, as well as direction, should come from the pastor in a spirit of enthusiasm and excitement. Leaders are revived and encouraged in the mother cell. In return, their revival and encouragement is caught by the rest of prayer cells.

4. Leaders Need to Ask Questions and Discuss Problems

The mother cell is an opportunity for the leader to learn from the experience and wisdom of the mother cell leader—the pastor. It also gives them an opportunity to learn from the experiences of other leaders. Each problem is different, but all problems share the same causes and cures.

5. There Should Be an Evaluation of What Is Taking Place in Each of the Prayer Cells

Leaders should give an account of the progress (or lack of it) in their cells. Suggestions may be made that will help steer the cells in the right direction. And suggestions may also be made that will help the leaders improve their leadership skills.

Also, the evaluation time can be a time of encouragement. For instance, the prayer cell leaders should bring their prayer request notebooks to this meeting. The reading of answered prayer requests can be a great source of encouragement to the other leaders and propel them on to even greater commitments to the purpose of the prayer cell strategy.

The discipleship cells (mother cells) can be structured so that the leaders will receive the broadest training possible. Below are examples of possible themes for six months of discipleship cells:

1. Power of God to answer prayer
2. Purpose and plan of prayer cells
3. Importance of the evangelism team
4. Christ's concern for the unsaved
5. Plan of accountability
6. A Bible study on the "Heart of a Leader"
7. Personal evangelism
8. Basic doctrine
9. Making God's Word yours
10. Pointing to the crusade
11. Altar work
12. Follow-up
13. How to pray for the unsaved
14. Maintaining personal spiritual focus
15. Spirit-filled life
16. Sanctify yourself/take up your cross
17. Power of faith
18. Developing faith
19. Praying in faith
20. Praying for healing
21. Praying for physical security, jobs, and finances
22. Praying for families
23. Praying for cell leaders

While the main purpose of the discipleship cell is discipling new leaders, there are other benefits as well. It builds a *team* that supports the successes (or setbacks) of each member. It also provides a sense of accountability. It is, in fact, crucial to the success of the system.

Benefits of a Prayer Cell

The list of the benefits a local church may derive from the cell strategy is great. Among the most important:

1. It stimulates the development of workers. They begin to discover their gifts and ministries.
2. The church and the pastor are decentralized.
3. Prayer is systematically offered for specific needs. James says, "When you ask, you do not receive, because you ask with wrong motives" (James 4:3).
4. There is growth in the local church. Participants of the cells will usually attend the mother church on Sunday.

Prayer cells can be used to prepare for evangelistic campaigns. Since it is recommended that local churches have an evangelistic campaign every six months, some pastors have found that it is natural to repeat the cycle of prayer cells on that same schedule.

112 VOLUNTEER MINISTRIES

Miscellaneous

1. Volunteer time in parachurch ministry (Prison Fellowship, Youth for Christ, Feed the Children, etc.).
2. Make safety contacts for shut-ins, elderly (phone call, visit).
3. Prayer (prayer partner, prayer chains, crisis).
4. Visitation (visit hospitalized or shut-in parishioners, local institutions).
5. Lead a support group (divorce recovery, grief recovery, parenting, financial management, etc.).
6. Teach a special needs class.
7. Take part in a community outreach event (marathon, snack booth).

Local Church

8. Cooking (prepare meals for church dinners and events, assist with daycare).
9. Communion assistant (prepare Communion elements for Communion service).
10. Server (dinners, receptions).
11. Building maintenance (repairs and maintains).
12. Vehicle maintenance (repairs and maintains).
13. Equipment maintenance (repairs and maintains).
14. Landscaping (planting, maintaining, trimming).
15. Remodeling (classrooms, auditoriums, meeting rooms).
16. Carpentry (church property, event staging).
17. Construction (building and renovation).
18. Contractor (supervise building and renovation projects).
19. Lawn care (planting, watering, mowing, raking).
20 Clear walks and driveways (snow removal, sweeping).
21. Set up/tear down (pre- and post-events).
22. Planning (architectural, programming, staffing, financial).
23. Driving (drive for church or daycare events).
24. Telephoning (make follow-up or reminder calls).
25. Mailing (bulletins, newsletters, advertising).
26. Cleaning (custodial).
27. Painting (church facilities).
28. Writing (worship folders, brochures, newsletters, blogs, letters, advertising).
29. Web design (church Web site, blogs).
30. Graphic design (worship folders, brochures, newsletters, advertising).
31. Printing (church publications, advertising, signage, ID badges).
32. Sewing (costumes, draperies).
33. Fund-raising (building projects, debt retirement, mission trips).
34. Woodworking (church or daycare furnishings).
35. Visiting (visitor follow-up, absentees).
36. Canvassing (outreach, church planting).
37. Accounting (church, departments, daycare, etc.).
38. Ushering (events, worship services).
39. Greeting (events, worship services).
40. Hosting (events, visitors, receptions).
41. Training (staff, new believers, membership).
42. Advertising (write copy and secure ad placement in local papers).

43. Marketing (assist with fund-raising, event participation, registration).
44. Plumbing (church properties).
45. Installing (carpeting, tiling, cabinetry).
46. Heating and cooling (church properties).
47. Acting (dramas, pageants, events, outreach).
48. Inspecting (safety, security, warranties).
49. Filing (records, books, teaching resources).
50. Counseling (church, outreach, compassionate ministries).
51. Electrical (installations, repairs).
52. Teaching (music, Bible classes, Vacation Bible School, student ministries).
53. Small groups (big brothers/big sisters, prayer cells, discipleship).
54. Speaking (events, clubs, and organizations).
55. Child care (events, worship services, training).
56. Daycare ministry (volunteer attendant, worker).
57. Librarian (church library).
58. Media director (distribute audiovisual equipment, file instructions and warranties).
59. Youth ministry (leader, sponsor, driver, host).
60. Young adult ministry (leader, event planner, sponsor, host).
61. Senior adult ministry and elder care (leader, event planner, host, driver).
62. Music (praise teams, choir, instrumentalist, set-up).
63. Drama (directing, costuming, make-up, coordinator).
64. Coach (recreational leagues, outreach).
65. Outreach (assist with events—planning and follow-up).
66. Office assistant (administrative assistant, receptionist, bookkeeper).
67. Technical support (computers, sound, lighting, taping).
68. Parking (direct traffic, greet visitors, report collisions).
69. Sign painting (property and event signage).
70. Decorating (seasonal, remodeling, building projects).
71. Dishwashing (events, dinners, receptions).
72. Clean-up (events, dinners, receptions).
73. Parish nursing (attend medical needs, provide nursing care on-site, in-home, education).
74. Security and safety (inspect facilities for health/safety hazards, secure buildings, patrol parking areas).
75. Retailing (operate church bookstore, kiosks).
76. Transportation (provide transportation for shut-ins, special needs).
77. Distribution (church flyers, advertisements).

Outreach

78. Bible study (start a neighborhood Bible study).
79. Community ministry (volunteering in a seasonal ministry).
80. Witness (give your testimony in worship service, outreach events).
81. Soul winning (learn and present soul winning presentation).
82. Blogging (start and maintain an outreach blog).
83. Athlete (participate in outreach sports).

Missions

84. Prayer support (enlist and participate in prayer missions and missionaries).
85. Support (conduct fund-raising for missions projects).
86. Team leader (organize and conduct overseas missions trips).
87. Communications (tape church events and send to missionaries).
88. Missions leader (teach about mission fields and missionaries).
89. Missions trips (participate in overseas missions trip).

Compassionate Ministries

90. Worship services (assist with worship services in missions and institutions).
91. Bible studies (teach a Bible class).
92. Food distribution (collect and distribute food goods).
93. Clothing distribution (collect and distribute clothing).
94. Evangelism and discipleship (assist with compassionate ministries outreach).
95. Health training (provide health and hygiene counseling).
96. Crisis pregnancy (assist expectant mothers, provide counseling, collect and distribute baby clothing and supplies).
97. Counseling services (provide volunteer counseling services to needy).
98. Legal services (provide volunteer legal services to needy).
99. Financial management training (assist needy with budgeting and financial planning).
100. Childcare (provide childcare for hospitalized, job seekers, imprisoned).
101. Eldercare (assist elderly with health, transportation, food services).
102. Recreation (provide organized recreation for inner-city children and youth).
103. Camping (provide camping experience for needy children and youth).
104. Job training (provide job skills training for unemployed).
105. Skills training (assist job seekers in improving job skills).
106. Women's shelters (operate or assist with shelter for abused).
107. Homeless care (provide health and hygiene supplies).
108. Parenting training (conduct seminars on parenting).
109. Medical clinics (organize and conduct authorized medical services).
110. ELL classes (teach English language learners).
111. Housing (provide temporary housing for displaced, homeless).
112. Transportation services (provide transportation for displaced, homeless).

SAMPLE DISCIPLER CERTIFICATE

Lake View Park
Church of the Nazarene

With God's help and the encouragement and support of my
local congregation, I, _____,
commit to not only winning at least one person to the Lord
but also discipling that person in 2007.

Each One Disciple One!

Signed: _____

APPENDIX L

FOLLOW-UP CHECKLIST

- ☐ Follow up weekly.
- ☐ Show updates weekly on how the church is doing.
- ☐ Introduce those involved in discipling new Christians to the congregation and include the new Christians in the introduction.
- ☐ Prepare a certificate recognizing the individuals who are discipling someone in the church. (See Appendix K for a sample certificate.)
- ☐ Schedule continuing prayer meetings.
- ☐ Have individuals share how God is blessing them through the discipling ministry.
- ☐ Explain on all occasions the plan of *Each One Disciple One*.

APPENDIX M

SAMPLE MEMBERSHIP CLASS OUTLINE

(Note: This is a partial version of the class outline. The complete outline is available on the *Each One Disciple One* CD.)

Belonging to the Lake View Park "Family Tree"

"I am the vine, you are the branches. If a man remains in me and I in him, he will bear much fruit; apart from me, you can do nothing."
John 15:5

"I am the Vine, you are the branches. When you're joined with me and I with you, the relation intimate and organic, the harvest is sure to be abundant. Separated, you can't produce a thing."
John 15:5 (TM)

Lake View Park Church of the Nazarene

Our Mission

We are a Christ-centered body of believers established on the Word of God, focused on the needs of our community and the world. We have no greater call than to know Him, to be known by Him, and to lead others to Him.

Our Vision

To be a New Testament church, fueled by prayer, fed by the Word of God, empowered by the Holy Spirit so that we might fulfill Scripture and see the Lord add to our number daily those who are being saved.

Goals for 2006

Children's Ministry
Financial Peace
Missions Focus
Renewal Focus
Facility Remodel

We must become a river and not a reservoir!

Leadership

Vision/mission
Preaching
Intern ministry
Mentoring leaders
Leadership training
Follow-up assimilation
Pastor's welcome class
Spiritual gifts discovery
Discipleship classes

Worship

Worship services
Music
Special celebrations
Baptism
Communion
Audiovisual
Decorations
Hospitality and all church dinner events

Stewardship

Budget preparation
Regulation and review
Recording and reporting
Audits
Stewardship emphasis
Fund-raising
Business operations
Counting teams
Financial contributions

Partnership

Building and Properties

Friendship

Prayer ministry
Encouragement
Evangelism (events and training)
Unchurched events

Fellowship

Sunday School ministry
Children
Youth (Nazarene Youth International)
Adults
Senior adults
Women's ministry
Men's ministry
Athletics
Weddings/showers
Missions (Nazarene Missions International)

Lake View Park's Core Values

1. We value the souls of lost people everywhere.
2. We value spending intimate time with a personal God in personal and corporate prayer.
3. We value the Word of God.
4. We value a lifestyle of holiness empowered by the Holy Spirit.
5. We value authentic relationship with God's family.
6. We value the worship of God, both personally and corporately.
7. We value the unique gifts of God's people.
8. We value personal integrity and honesty.

Our Statement of Belief

Lake View Park is a member of the Church of the Nazarene. We have 16 Articles of Faith. These statements are given in their completeness in our church *Manual.* It takes many hours of intense study to understand all the theological terms used in the Articles of Faith. Because a statement of doctrine is meant to last for many generations, it is necessary to present it in the precise and technical language of theology. Here is a summary of these 16 statements:

1. We believe in one God, the Creator of all things, who reveals himself as Father, Son, and Spirit. (Triune God)

2. We believe in Jesus Christ, who is fully God and fully human at the same time, who became like us to bring about our salvation. (Jesus Christ)

3. We believe in the Holy Spirit, who is active in the world, bringing man to salvation. (The Holy Spirit)

4. We believe that the Bible is the Word of God, giving us all we need to know about how to be saved. (The Holy Scriptures)

5. We believe that we are all sinners by both nature and act and need God's forgiveness and cleansing. (Sin, Original and Personal)

6. We believe that Jesus Christ died on the Cross and that, trusting in His death, we can be restored to right relationship with God. (Atonement)

7. We believe that God has enabled us to turn to Him from sin, but that He has not forced us to do so. (Prevenient Grace)

8. We believe that individually we must repent, turn away from our sins, and trust Christ to accept us. (Repentance)

9. We believe that when we turn from sin and trust in Christ, the old record of sin is wiped clean, and we are born anew, thus becoming part of the family of God. (Justification, Regeneration, Adoption)

10. We believe that after being born anew, we need the fullness of God's Spirit in our hearts. When we make a complete commitment to Him (consecration), He cleanses our spirit, fills us with His perfect love, and gives us the power to live victoriously. (Sanctification)

11. We believe in the Church, the community that confesses Jesus Christ as Lord. (Church)

12. We believe in baptism and urge people to be baptized as Christians. (Baptism)

13. We believe in the Lord's Supper. (Lord's Supper)

14. We believe God can heal. We pray for healing. We also believe that God can work through medical science. (Divine Healing)

15. We believe that Jesus Christ is coming again. (Second Coming)

16. We believe that everyone shall face the judgment of God with its rewards and punishments. (Resurrection, Judgment and Destiny)

A statement of belief has little value without the action of believing.

To believe is to trust God, to trust Him with complete obedience.

NOTES

1. Wording for the Lord's Prayer is from *The 1979 U. S. Book of Common Prayer* (1979; Justus.anglican.org, 1993), 54, http://justus.anglican.org/resources/bcp/bcp79.pdf (accessed January 30, 2008).

2. Samuel Logan Brengle, "How to Study the Bible" <http://foru.ms/t3853823-how-to-study-the-bible-by-samuel-logan-brengle.html>.

3. Ibid.

4. Merriam-Webster Online <http://m-w.com/dictionary/worship>.

5. "Sacrament," Merriam-Webster Online <http://www.m-w.com/dictionary/sacraments>.

6. *JESUS Film* Harvest Partners. Available at <http://www.jfhp.org/progress/popstory.cfm?storiesUID=258>.

7. Joel Comiskey, "Truth and Myth about Evangelism and Community: How Small Group Community and Mission Fit Together" Available at <http://www.joelcomiskeygroup.com/articles/evangelism/TruthMythEvangelism.htm>.

8. Bill and Amy Stearns, *2020 Vision* (Minneapolis: Bethany House, 2005), 15-16.

9. Oswald Chambers, *My Utmost for His Highest* (Uhrichsville, Ohio: Barbour and Company, 1963 by Oswald Chambers Publications, Ltd.), 194.

10. *Cambridge Dictionary,* "Relationship" <http://dictionary.cambridge.org/define.asp?key=66631&dict=CALD>.

11. "Infant Development: What Happens from Birth to 3 Months" <http:www.cnn.com/HEALTH/library/PR/00061.html>.

12. H. Orton Wiley, "The Person and Work of the Holy Spirit," Online <http://wesley.nnu.edu/holiness_tradition/wiley/wiley-2-25.htm>.

13. John Mason, *The Impossible Is Possible* (Minneapolis: Bethany House, 2003), 63.

14. Chambers, *My Utmost for His Highest,* 194.

15. "Infant Development: What Happens from Birth to 3 Months" <http:www.cnn.com/HEALTH/library/PR/00061.html>.

16. Chambers, *My Utmost for His Highest,* 194.

17. "Infant Development: What Happens from birth to 3 months" <http:www.cnn.com/HEALTH/library/PR/00061.html>.